The Joy of Being Loved

by the Creator of the Universe and the
Greatest Lover of all Time!

A 31-Day Devotional and Journaling
Encounter Based on the Song of Songs

Denise Siemens

"This is a beautiful book with a beautiful theme, *The Joy of Being Loved*! You will want to take time and pray through this insightful devotional. I can promise you, a greater joy in the love of God is about to come upon you as you read this book. Denise Siemens has given us an open door into the fire and beauty of God's love. It will touch areas of your heart you may have never known were even there. Pick up a copy for a friend and watch them enter into *"The Joy of Being Loved!"*

Brian Simmons
Passion & Fire Ministries
The Passion Translation Project

If there is anyone who has had continual revelation of God's love by studying the Song of Solomon it is Denise Siemens. She has combined her knowledge of scripture and understanding of the Father's love to write this beautiful 31-day devotional. Because of this devotional, the Song of Songs has become a go-to book for in-depth understanding of God's daily love for me. There is no love that can compare to God's fiery passionate love.

J.D. Hershberger
Minister of Worship
Kingdom Life Ministries

In 2008 I asked God for "more," and I would sit quietly before Him on a daily basis as He unpacked my life. When I received *The Joy of Being Loved* devotional this year, it was like reading the conversations Jesus and I had from 2008 to this present day. This devotional is so anointed that each time I read it I weep. Not tears of sadness, but tears of joy because when I'm done, I truly feel I've been with Jesus.

Barbara Woodruff
God Encounter Facilitator

Thank You

Thank you to my amazing husband, Allen, who continually encouraged me and helped in the editing. Thank you to our daughter, Annie Eklov, for her passionate love of the Bridegroom God that stirred a holy jealousy in me for more. Thank you to Kelsey Vine for the many ways that she has helped in editing and encouraging. Thank you to Katie Palani for her work on the cover and Sagar Palani for the picture on the back. Thank you to Mike Bickle, Rhonda Calhoun and Dr. Brian Simmons whose teachings on the Song of Songs have caused me to fall deeper in love with my Bridegroom God. Thank you to many others who also prayed, encouraged and edited. What a blessing! Thank you!

Dedication

Jesus, my Bridegroom King, You overwhelm me! I cry out for more! I long for more of Your holy kisses, more of Your fiery passionate love, more of You! You have overcome me with one glance of Your eyes! I must have You, and I cannot live without You. I love You with a fiery passionate burning heart of love. I say, "Yes," to your seal of fiery flames upon my heart and Your seal of blazing passion covering my entire being. May each one who reads this devotional fall more in love with You, and may their hearts burn continually with fiery passion for You, Jesus, becoming one with YOU. May they experience *The Joy of Being Loved* by You in a deeper way than they've ever known. May they discover who they are as they see who You are! May they discover their purpose, destiny and vision in You as they become one with You. May You be their VISION! Thank You, Jesus, for Your amazing, extravagant love! Thank You for all that You've done for me! You are everything I've ever wanted, everything I've ever needed and everything I've ever desired! You are my everything! This is Your love story, Yeshua, Your love song, the greatest song ever sung! I love You forever and always, and I dedicate this devotional to YOU, my Bridegroom King.

Introduction

Welcome!

Welcome! Welcome to the greatest adventure of all time! Be prepared to fall in love with our Bridegroom God again and again. God's Word and His Spirit will transform your life as you open up your heart and welcome His healing love into the deepest places!

Purpose

The purpose of this devotional is for you to receive the truth of our Bridegroom God's love for you in a deeper way, falling more in love with Him, so that you can receive His freedom, His healing, His identity, HIs vision and His destiny for your life. The Lord is calling His Bride to awaken and to mature in His love in this hour of history. As you read this devotional, may the Lord ignite a fiery passionate love, hunger and thirst in your entire being for Him that will propel you into depths in God that you've never known!

It's All About Him and His Love!

This love story in the Song of Songs is all about our Bridegroom King and His love for you! We love Him, only because He first loved us (I John 4:19). You were created for love! His story, HISTORY, is all about LOVE. All of history is moving toward a wedding - the most epic and the most beautiful wedding of all time (Rev. 19:6-9)! It's all about our Bridegroom God and His desire to invite us into the divine dance, the divine romance of His love and communion with Him.

The Greatest Love Story

Jesus' love story is the greatest love story ever told and the most epic love song ever sung. It is the Song of all Songs - the supreme love song, just as Jesus is the King of all Kings - the Supreme King. His amazing love song will take you into the Holy of Holies - the secret place in His heart where your heart beats as ONE with HIS. You will be transformed as you rest in His love. Jesus came to set you free from all ungodly fear by loving you to maturity. It's His beautiful love that will heal you, transform you and set you free.

Characters of the Song of Songs

King Solomon wrote the Song of Songs. This eight chapter love song is a natural love story about Solomon's love for a shepherdess, but it also represents a deeper spiritual meaning. In this allegory, King Solomon represents Jesus, the Bridegroom, and the shepherdess represents you, the Bride. It is a beautiful story about Jesus joyfully loving His Bride (us) into maturity. The Bride overcomes fear because of the Bridegroom's extravagant love and grows in holy passion for Him. *This love relationship with Christ is an intimate spiritual relationship, not physical.* The first time the shepherdess is called the Bride is in the middle of the Song. However, for purposes of clarity, she will be called the Bride throughout this devotional. Yeshua, Jesus' Hebrew name, is used interchangeably with Jesus in this book.

Biblical Support

There are many scriptures throughout the Bible that support the view of a Bridegroom God. In John 3:29, John the Baptist calls Jesus the Bridegroom. In Matthew 9:15, Jesus refers to Himself as the Bridegroom. Revelation 19:6-9 gives us a picture of the Wedding Supper of the Lamb. In the last chapter of the Bible, in Revelation 22:17, it says, "The Spirit and the bride say, 'Come.'" Our identity at the end of the age will be that of a Bride who's lovesick and longing for her Bridegroom. There are many other references throughout the Bible concerning the Bridegroom God and His Bride which support the allegorical interpretation of Song of Songs. You are encouraged to check it out in the Word.

An Invitation to Encounter the Bridegroom God

You have an invitation to encounter and experience the love of the Bridegroom God and oneness with Him in a greater way than ever before. There is no end to the width, length, depth and height of God's love - there's always more! Saying, "Yes," to His invitation will propel you into glorious realms of His beautiful heart and communion with Him. Don't miss the greatest treasure hunt of all time. Don't miss the most fascinating song of love ever written, for this love song is meant for you!

He's Real

As you read this Song of Songs devotional, let the Bridegroom King be real to you and encounter the God of Glory each day, meeting Him in your cleansed imagination! Jesus told us in Matt. 22:37 to, "Love the Lord your God with all your heart...soul and...mind." One definition of mind in this verse is imagination. Jesus wants us to love Him with our all, including all our imagination! He wants to be real to you. Using all five of your spiritual senses, see His beautiful face and look into His eyes of love. Hear His voice as He speaks to you and sings over you. Feel His healing love through hugs and touch. Breathe in the fragrance of His intoxicating perfume and taste His delicious goodness. He's real. Experience the joy of being loved by our Bridegroom God!

Simple Steps to Encountering God

Encounter Him as you read each day's devotion. Ask Him to cleanse your imagination with His blood and to open your spiritual senses - the eyes, ears, etc. of your heart so that you can connect with Him in a way that is real and meaningful to you (Eph. 1:18, Rev. 2:7, Ps. 34:8, II Cor. 2:15). Go to a safe place in your imagination and meet Him there. Let Him share His heart with you as you read the devotion. Share your heart with Him. Write down what you see, hear, feel, taste and smell in the spiritual realm as you meet with Him. Experience the joy of a loving relationship with Jesus as you encounter His cherishing heart for you! Please see the following page for a sample prayer outline that you can use each day to prepare you to meet with the Bridegroom King after reading the devotion.

Sample Outline

Below is an example you can use each day to prepare your heart for an intentional encounter with God as you read this devotional. There are no formulas, so allow the Lord to lead you.

Calling my spirit to attention: Spirit, I bless you to rise up in all God's glory and to commune with the Holy Spirit, following His lead and taking your seat in the heavenlies. Spirit, I bless you to be flooded with God's love, joy, and peace, receiving truth and revelation from His heart. Body and soul, I bless you to rest, relax and receive all that the Lord has for you as you follow the lead of the Holy Spirit.

Prayer: Lord, I love you, and I'm hungry for more. I want to meet with you today, encountering you in your Word, in Spirit and in Truth.

Thank you, Jesus, for all that you did for me on the cross. Thank You for Your death and resurrection power! Thank You for Your great love for me! Thank You for choosing me. I choose You!

Jesus, I repent for any way that I have allowed ungodly pictures and thoughts to enter in and dwell in me. I ask Your forgiveness. Thank You for coming now and cleansing and purifying my mind, my thoughts and my imagination with Your all powerful blood.   Come and fill me with Your thoughts and Your pictures.

Thank You for cleansing all the doorways in my spirit, soul and body with Your blood and flooding them with Your light, life and love. I invite You to be my doorkeeper at every doorway.

Thank You, Father, Jesus and Holy Spirit that You want to be real to me. Come and meet me now in a safe place, a place of Your beauty and glory, a place of Your love, peace and joy where we can commune together and share the secrets of our hearts with one another. Amen.

Note: Your safe place may be a garden, a beach, your home, a meadow, etc. Once in your safe place, ask the Lord to come. Look for Him and thank Him for coming. Share your heart with Him and listen to His heart. If you choose, you may ask the Lord the questions listed for that day and record your encounter on the pages following each devotional. Let your heart overflow with the joy of being loved!

Day 1

"Let him kiss me..." SS 1:2 (NIV)

Bride: Heavenly Father, Papa, let your Son, let the Bridegroom King, kiss my heart with the kisses of His Word, for every word that proceeds from His mouth brings life to my innermost being and light to my path. Let Him kiss me alive with the breath of His Spirit upon my heart. Let Him kiss me with the intimate holy kisses of His Living Word, bringing revelation that washes and purifies me. Let Him kiss me with His cherishing love! My heart cries out for more. I have experienced His affectionate heart, and it has caused me to fall head-over-heels in love with Him. I must have more of His kisses! Let Him kiss me...

Papa: My Dearest Daughter, whom I love with great joy, you are so right to ask to "let Him" kiss you. It's so right for you to rest in His love with a yielded heart, letting Him love you with His kisses. You don't need to strive or to work. All you need do is "let Him." As you agree with Him and say, "Yes," to Him, open your heart to receive the kisses of His Word, for His Word is life, and allow Him to do the work that will conform you to His image. You are my Son's glorious and delightful inheritance! It is right for you to cry out for His kisses, for My heart for My Son is that He would have a people, a Bride, fully yielded and fully in love with Him. I want My Son to have a passionate fiery Bride who looks like Him and is equally yoked to Him. My Son and I love you beyond your wildest imagination! I loved you and everyone in the world so very much that I held nothing back, not even My precious Son. I asked the One Whom I treasure and cherish with all my heart, and, in Whom I delight, to come and rescue and save you that you would not perish but have eternal life. He loved you so much that He came to earth as a man. Jesus, my Son, humbled Himself and became obedient to death on a cross because of His great love for you. Our love for you is wider, longer, higher and deeper than you can comprehend. Open wide your heart and receive His love and His kisses. Let My Son love you. Let My Son kiss you! My Son's heart beats wildly with love for you! Let Him...and He will...

Scripture Reading: SS 1:1-4 (tPt); Eph. 1:18, 3:18; Rom. 8:29; John 3:16; Phil. 2:8; Matt. 4:4

Encounter the Bridegroom God

Encounter the Bridegroom King as you read today's devotion (see Simple Steps to Encountering God and Sample Outline in Introduction). Continue your encounter with the Lord in your safe place. Journal as you share your hearts with one another.

Safe Place (describe)

_____

_____

_____

Papa, would you give me a picture of how much you love me?

_____

_____

_____

_____

_____

_____

Would you show me how much Jesus, the Bridegroom, loves me?

_____

_____

_____

_____

_____

Papa, how do I open up my heart and receive Jesus' love and kisses?

_____

_____

_____

_____

_____

_____

Thank You for meeting me here today, Papa! Thank You for all that you did. Thank You for your love! Thank You for...

_____

_____

_____

What truths are the Bridegroom/Papa/Holy Spirit speaking over you today? Write down these truths and speak them out loud as you see these truths in your imagination (i.e. He calls you beautiful, so see yourself as beautiful as you say out loud, "I'm beautiful!").

_____
_____
_____
_____
_____
_____
_____

What lies have you been believing? Ask the Lord to set you free from any deception and then focus on the Lord and His truth. Agree with God, and declare His life over you, as you speak/sing His truth.

_____
_____
_____
_____
_____
_____

How does the Bridegroom God feel about you? See you?

_____
_____
_____
_____
_____
_____
_____

Who do you say the Lord is? (Matt. 16:13) Who you believe God to be will affect every area of your walk with Him. Speak the truth and see it!

_____
_____
_____
_____
_____
_____
_____

Who does the Lord say you are? What's the truth about your identity and your destiny? What you believe about yourself will affect every area of your walk with Him. Speak the truth out loud and see it.

_____

_____

_____

_____

_____

_____

_____

_____

How has the Lord shown you His extravagant love and how has He kissed you today?

_____

_____

_____

_____

_____

_____

_____

_____

_____

_____

Worship Him and thank Him for Who He is! Let your heart overflow with the joy of being loved!

_____

_____

_____

_____

_____

_____

_____

_____

_____

_____

Arise, My Bride, and walk in your destiny! It's a new day!

Day 2

"Let him kiss me with the kisses of his mouth - for your love is more delightful than wine." SS 1:2 (NIV)

Bride: Kiss me with the kisses of Your Word - Your Words of affirmation, identity, truth and love. Your Words to me are more precious than gold, than much pure gold, and they are sweeter than honey. Your Words bring light to my darkness and wisdom and joy to my life. Kiss me with Your kisses of revelation knowledge, that I might know Your love for me in a greater way! Kiss me, my Bridegroom King, with the kisses of Your heart - with the kisses of holy intimacy - You in me and me in You! I long to know the deepest things of Your heart, my King! I long for Your kisses, Yeshua, for Your kisses are more pleasurable than any delight. I must have more of You! I'm desperate! I'm lovesick for You, Jesus! Kiss me with the kisses of Your touch - Your hand on my heart! Kiss me with Your fiery passionate love, that I might burn brighter for You! I long for Your kisses, for Your love is greater than, more beautiful than, and more delightful than anything this world has to offer. The things of this world that I once considered valuable, I now consider worthless for the surpassing greatness of knowing You, my Beautiful King. You are more precious than all this world has to offer, and nothing I desire compares with You. I love You! Kiss me…

Bridegroom: Open wide the door of your heart and receive My kisses! Receive My love, My joy and My delight over you! For you are the love of My life! You are the one I desire and long for. I love you, My Darling, with all My heart, with all My mind, with all My soul and with all My strength. It's true! I'm lovesick for you! Receive My love. You were made for love! You were created for love! Just let Me love you and receive! Nothing will satisfy or heal you like My love and affection and the truth of My Word. Read My Living Word and receive My kisses of love. You are the joy of My life, and I will cherish you forever!

Scripture Reading: SS 1:1-4 (NIV); Phil. 3:7-8; Heb. 12:1-3; Prov. 8:11; Ps. 19:10

Encounter the Bridegroom God

Encounter the Bridegroom King as you read today's devotion (see Simple Steps to Encountering God and Sample Outline in Introduction). Continue your encounter with the Lord in your safe place. Journal as you share your hearts with one another.

Safe Place (describe)

_____

_____

_____

Can you picture Yeshua's arms open to you and can you run into His embrace of love and let Him hold you?

_____

_____

_____

_____

_____

_____

Jesus, do You really love me with Your all - all Your heart, soul, mind and strength?

_____

_____

_____

_____

_____

_____

_____

Can you help me to feel and perceive Your love for me? I want to know in my knower Your great love for me personally.

_____

_____

_____

Thank You, Jesus, for meeting me here today! Thank You for...

_____

_____

_____

What truths are the Bridegroom/Papa/Holy Spirit speaking over you today? Write down these truths and speak them out loud as you see these truths in your imagination (i.e. He calls you beautiful, so see yourself as beautiful as you say out loud, "I'm beautiful!").

_____

_____

_____

_____

_____

_____

_____

What lies have you been believing? Ask the Lord to set you free from any deception and then focus on the Lord and His truth. Agree with God, and declare His life over you, as you speak/sing His truth.

_____

_____

_____

_____

_____

_____

_____

How does the Bridegroom God feel about you? See you?

_____

_____

_____

_____

_____

_____

_____

Who do you say the Lord is? (Matt. 16:13) Who you believe God to be will affect every area of your walk with Him. Speak the truth and see it!

_____

_____

_____

_____

_____

_____

_____

Who does the Lord say you are? What's the truth about your identity and your destiny? What you believe about yourself will affect every area of your walk with Him. Speak the truth out loud and see it.

_____

_____

_____

_____

_____

_____

_____

_____

How has the Lord shown you His extravagant love and how has He kissed you today?

_____

_____

_____

_____

_____

_____

_____

_____

_____

Worship Him and thank Him for Who He is! Let your heart overflow with the joy of being loved!

_____

_____

_____

_____

_____

_____

_____

_____

_____

_____

_____

_____

Arise, My Bride, and walk in your destiny! It's a new beginning!

Day 3

"Draw me after you and let us run together!" SS 1:4 (NASB)

Bride: Draw me into intimacy, Yeshua, into a heavenly oneness with You, and let us run together in anointed ministry.

Bridegroom: I have drawn you with lovingkindness and loved you with an everlasting love. I'm wooing you because you are the apple of My eye. You are the one I love - My favorite. You are valuable, unique and significant. My love for you is as great as My Father's love for Me. And My Heavenly Father loves you the same as He loves Me! Isn't that amazing? Do you not know? Have you not heard? Can you not see? You are loved with the greatest love possible! You are loved the same way that God loves God! You are priceless and precious. I created you for love. I am drawing you to My heart that we may be one and run together in anointed ministry to share My love with a hurting world. I love you, My Darling, My Lover Friend, and I love how you love Me. I'm drawing you with wide open arms. Come into the chambers of My heart and spend time with Me. Open wide the doors of your heart and receive My love, for you will only love Me to the degree that you know I love you. Come, deeper still in My love, My Darling, and let us run together in My glory. Let us minister healing rivers of life and love to the wounded and hurting! Come! I'm drawing you with My lovingkindness so that we can run together.

Scripture Reading: SS 1:1-4 (NASB); Jer. 31:3b; John 15:9,17:23; Zech. 2:8

Encounter the Bridegroom God

Encounter the Bridegroom King as you read today's devotion (see Simple Steps to Encountering God and Sample Outline in Introduction). Continue your encounter with the Lord in your safe place. Journal as you share your hearts with one another.

Safe Place (describe)

_____
_____
_____

Father, how much do you love Your Son, Jesus?

_____
_____
_____
_____
_____
_____

Father, how much do you love me?

_____
_____
_____
_____
_____
_____

Jesus, why am I Your favorite? What do you love about me?

_____
_____
_____
_____
_____

Thank You, Bridegroom God, for Your love. Thank you for...

_____
_____
_____

What truths are the Bridegroom/Papa/Holy Spirit speaking over you today? Write down these truths and speak them out loud as you see these truths in your imagination (i.e. He calls you beautiful, so see yourself as beautiful as you say out loud, "I'm beautiful!").

_____
_____
_____
_____
_____
_____
_____

What lies have you been believing? Ask the Lord to set you free from any deception and then focus on the Lord and His truth. Agree with God, and declare His life over you, as you speak/sing His truth.

_____
_____
_____
_____
_____
_____
_____

How does the Bridegroom God feel about you? See you?

_____
_____
_____
_____
_____
_____
_____

Who do you say the Lord is? (Matt. 16:13) Who you believe God to be will affect every area of your walk with Him. Speak the truth and see it!

_____
_____
_____
_____
_____
_____
_____

Who does the Lord say you are? What's the truth about your identity and your destiny? What you believe about yourself will affect every area of your walk with Him. Speak the truth out loud and see it.

_____
_____
_____
_____
_____
_____
_____
_____

How has the Lord shown you His extravagant love and how has He kissed you today?

_____
_____
_____
_____
_____
_____
_____
_____

Worship Him and thank Him for Who He is! Let your heart overflow with the joy of being loved!

_____
_____
_____
_____
_____
_____
_____
_____
_____
_____
_____

Arise, My Bride, and walk in your destiny! It's a new day dawning!

Day 4

"I know I am so unworthy - so in need..."
SS 1:5b (tPt)

Bride: I am so unworthy - so needy. I have failed so often and in so many ways that I can't believe anyone would want me or love me. My heart is dry, and I am dark.

Bridegroom: My Bride, you are lovely! I focus on your loveliness not your darkness. Your dream for love has come true! Open the doors of your heart wide to receive all My tender affectionate love for you. You are not an accident or a mistake. You are not a failure! That is not who you are. You are my child and you are loved. I created you on purpose for a purpose and I love you! I created you for love. I'm knocking, waiting and longing for a deeper more intimate relationship with you. Open up and invite me in to light up every area of your heart and to feast with you. There is no condemnation for those who are found in Me and Me in them. Don't hold back. Don't close Me off or put up a wall. This has nothing to do with your worth! You will never be good enough! You can't do it! This has nothing to do with you but has everything to do with Me! You must know that I did it all for you and for My Father! I did it all for love! I loved you so much that I said, "Yes," to My Father! I went to the cross and took care of everything! All you need to do is say, "Yes," to me! My blood paid the price. It was a high cost! It cost Me everything, My very life! But you are worth it all to Me! You mean everything to Me! You were the joy set before Me and the reason I endured the cross. I love you! I cherish you! Your dream for love has come true! This is true love…this is true JOY!

Scripture Reading: SS 1:5-11 (tPt); Rev. 3:20; Heb. 12:1-3; Rom. 8:1

Encounter the Bridegroom God

Encounter the Bridegroom King as you read today's devotion (see Simple Steps to Encountering God and Sample Outline in Introduction). Continue your encounter with the Lord in your safe place. Journal as you share your hearts with one another.

Safe Place (describe)

_____
_____
_____

Jesus, would You give me a picture of what I mean to You?

_____
_____
_____
_____

Yeshua, is there a dark, dry place in my heart that You would like to shine Your light on and heal?

_____
_____
_____
_____

Help me, Jesus, to feel the safety of Your love and to say "Yes" to Your searchlight of love shining in the dry, dark places of my heart.

_____
_____
_____

Bridegroom King, how do you see me? Help me to see myself the way You see me.

_____
_____
_____

Thank You, Jesus, for Your gentleness and Your kindness. Thank You for focusing on my loveliness and not my darkness. Thank You for...

_____
_____

What truths are the Bridegroom/Papa/Holy Spirit speaking over you today? Write down these truths and speak them out loud as you see these truths in your imagination (i.e. He calls you beautiful, so see yourself as beautiful as you say out loud, "I'm beautiful!").

_____
_____
_____
_____
_____
_____
_____

What lies have you been believing? Ask the Lord to set you free from any deception and then focus on the Lord and His truth. Agree with God, and declare His life over you, as you speak/sing His truth.

_____
_____
_____
_____
_____
_____
_____

How does the Bridegroom God feel about you? See you?

_____
_____
_____
_____
_____
_____
_____

Who do you say the Lord is? (Matt. 16:13) Who you believe God to be will affect every area of your walk with Him. Speak the truth and see it!

_____
_____
_____
_____
_____
_____
_____

Who does the Lord say you are? What's the truth about your identity and your destiny? What you believe about yourself will affect every area of your walk with Him. Speak the truth out loud and see it.

_____
_____
_____
_____
_____
_____
_____
_____
_____
_____

How has the Lord shown you His extravagant love and how has He kissed you today?

_____
_____
_____
_____
_____
_____
_____
_____
_____
_____
_____

Thank Him and worship Him for Who He is! Enjoy the joy of being loved!

_____
_____
_____
_____
_____
_____
_____
_____

Arise, My Bride, and walk in your destiny! It's a new day!

Day 5

"I am dark, but lovely..." SS 1:5 (NIV)

Bride: I am dark, but lovely. What a revelation! I am so weak but I know that I am still Yours and that You still love me in spite of all my faults. I know I sin, but You are ravished over me! Whenever I blow it, I can run into Your arms, Yeshua, repent and receive Your forgiveness. You always accept me and will never reject me. What freedom and security Your love brings! I don't have to fear You or run away from You! You are a good, good God! I can't help falling in love with You, especially when I see Your love and acceptance of me no matter what! I love You only because You first loved me! I delight in You only because You first delighted in me! Knowing how You love me makes me want to please You more. Jesus, I desire to delight in the Spirit of the Fear of the Lord! I don't want anything in me that is not of You! Help me overcome! I know Your love for me will never change! I love You and I long to be just like You!

Bridegroom: Yes, My Darling, I know all about you. I know all about your loveliness, and I know all about your darkness. I still love you and always will. I knew when you first came to Me that you were not mature and that it would take time for you to grow up. I knew it would be a process. I have enjoyed every stage! You delight My heart, My Love, and I want you to know and feel the delight that I have over you! I see the, "Yes," in your spirit towards Me, and I am thrilled! I love you right now, right where you're at, and I'm not changing My mind about you! The truth is that you need to know that I think you're lovely even though, at the same time, I see the darkness in your heart. Unless you understand how I see you and love you in spite of those areas that you struggle in, you will not be able to grow spiritually. I'm a good God and I rejoice in doing you good! I'm faithful to complete that which I've begun in you. I love you so much that I'm calling you to come up higher in Me and walk in my righteousness. The truth is that you can't do anything to make Me love you any more or any less. I just love you. So, My Dear, be filled with My love and delight over you, and joy will flood your soul!

Scripture Reading: SS 1:5-11 (NIV); Jer. 32:38-41; I John 4:18; Eph. 2:4-5; Phil. 1:6

Encounter the Bridegroom God

Encounter the Bridegroom King as you read today's devotion (see Simple Steps to Encountering God and Sample Outline in Introduction). Continue your encounter with the Lord in your safe place. Journal as you share your hearts with one another.

Safe Place (describe)

_____

_____

_____

Lord, how do you see the dark places of my heart?

_____

_____

_____

Jesus, help me to feel your love as we look at my heart together.

_____

_____

_____

_____

Bridegroom King, how can you completely love and accept me in spite of my struggles and sin?

_____

_____

_____

_____

Yeshua, what does true freedom look like?

_____

_____

_____

_____

Thank You that You're a good, good Father and that you rejoice in doing me good! Thank You that You are faithful to complete that which You've begun in me. Thank You for...

_____

_____

What truths are the Bridegroom/Papa/Holy Spirit speaking over you today? Write down these truths and speak them out loud as you see these truths in your imagination (i.e. He calls you beautiful, so see yourself as beautiful as you say out loud, "I'm beautiful!").

_____

_____

_____

_____

_____

_____

_____

What lies have you been believing? Ask the Lord to set you free from any deception and then focus on the Lord and His truth. Agree with God, and declare His life over you, as you speak/sing His truth.

_____

_____

_____

_____

_____

_____

How does the Bridegroom God feel about you? See you?

_____

_____

_____

_____

_____

_____

_____

Who do you say the Lord is? (Matt. 16:13) Who you believe God to be will affect every area of your walk with Him. Speak the truth and see it!

_____

_____

_____

_____

_____

_____

_____

Who does the Lord say you are? What's the truth about your identity and your destiny? What you believe about yourself will affect every area of your walk with Him. Speak the truth out loud and see it.

_____
_____
_____
_____
_____
_____
_____
_____

How has the Lord shown you His extravagant love and how has He kissed you today?

_____
_____
_____
_____
_____
_____
_____
_____
_____

Thank Him and worship Him for Who He is!

_____
_____
_____
_____
_____
_____
_____
_____
_____
_____
_____
_____

Arise, My Bride, and walk in your destiny! It's a new day!

Day 6

"How beautiful you are, my darling! Oh, how beautiful! Your eyes are doves."
SS 1:15 (NIV)

Bridegroom: Oh, My Dearest Darling, you are so beautiful! You are so lovely and amazing. You are beautiful beyond compare. Your eyes are doves eyes! You focus on Me without distraction! You have eyes for only Me, and you gaze into My eyes with such tender love and devotion. Your eyes are a feast for Me, and I drink them in. My heart overflows with joy as I gaze into your beautiful eyes and receive all that you have to give Me. As you continue to behold Me, keeping your focus on Me, I will transform you from glory to glory. I'm so in love with you, my Beautiful One!

Bride: Oh, my Bridegroom King, You see me like that when I am so easily distracted? There is no condemnation for how often I've looked away from You? Wow! You love me just like I am! Could this really be true? Oh, how I want to believe it! You are beautiful and glorious! You are all powerful, the most excellent of men! I must have more of you. Your eyes are like blazing fire, and Your voice like the sound of mighty rushing waters. You shine like the sun in all it's dazzling brilliance! Everyone who knows You thinks You're the best! There is none like You. Thank You for the way You see me! You have dove's eyes, my Bridegroom King! Your gaze upon me never waivers, and it never ends! Your love pours forth from Your passionate fiery eyes into my eyes and into my heart! You are the burning passionate One who boils over, and, looking at You causes my heart to boil over as well. You are so easy to love! When I look in Your eyes I'm drawn with holy desire. As I see the love in Your eyes, feel the love in Your touch, hear the love in Your words, encountering You, I can't help myself! Your merciful love and life-giving truth have set me free! You are the Beautiful One! I find myself falling, falling, falling more in love with You. Here I come, my Beautiful King of Glory!

Scripture Reading: SS 1:12-17; Rev. 1:14-16; Is. 4:2; John 8:32; 2 Cor. 3:18

Encounter the Bridegroom God

Encounter the Bridegroom King as you read today's devotion (see Simple Steps to Encountering God and Sample Outline in Introduction). Continue your encounter with the Lord in your safe place. Journal as you share your hearts with one another.

Safe Place (describe)

_____
_____
_____

Jesus, do You really love me just like I am?

_____
_____
_____
_____
_____

As I gaze into Your eyes of love I see...

_____
_____
_____
_____

As I sense the love in Your touch I feel...

_____
_____
_____
_____

As I hear the love in Your words I discover...

_____
_____
_____
_____

Thank You for the way You see me. Thank You for the way You love me. Thank You for...

_____
_____

What truths are the Bridegroom/Papa/Holy Spirit speaking over you today? Write down these truths and speak them out loud as you see these truths in your imagination (i.e. He calls you beautiful, so see yourself as beautiful as you say out loud, "I'm beautiful!").

_____
_____
_____
_____
_____
_____
_____

What lies have you been believing? Ask the Lord to set you free from any deception and then focus on the Lord and His truth. Agree with God, and declare His life over you, as you speak/sing His truth.

_____
_____
_____
_____
_____
_____
_____

How does the Bridegroom God feel about you? See you?

_____
_____
_____
_____
_____
_____
_____

Who do you say the Lord is? (Matt. 16:13) Who you believe God to be will affect every area of your walk with Him. Speak the truth and see it!

_____
_____
_____
_____
_____
_____
_____

Who does the Lord say you are? What's the truth about your identity and your destiny? What you believe about yourself will affect every area of your walk with Him. Speak the truth out loud and see it.

_____
_____
_____
_____
_____
_____
_____
_____
_____
_____
_____

How has the Lord shown you His extravagant love and how has He kissed you today?

_____
_____
_____
_____
_____
_____
_____
_____
_____
_____
_____

Worship Him and thank Him for Who He is! Delight in the joy of being loved!

_____
_____
_____
_____
_____
_____
_____
_____

Arise, My Bride, in the joy of My love and walk in your destiny!

Day 7

"I am truly his rose, the very theme of his song..." SS 2:1 (tPt)

Bride: I finally know who I am! I now know my identity! I'm Your inheritance, Yeshua! I'm Your rose and Your lily, and I'm overshadowed by Your chuppah glory - Your wedding canopy! I'm overshadowed by Your love! I'm the object of Your affection! I'm Your Bride! And I know and believe it now. I'm worthy because You have made me worthy! I choose to believe the truth! I'm the one You cherish, the one You see as pure and lovely. I'm Your very song, the one You are singing over with great joy! You flood my heart with love song after love song, drawing me to You. I can't resist You any longer! I can hear You now! Your voice is so sweet and Your love song so powerful as the melody of Your undying love washes over me and draws me into your heart! I can see You now! You are full of splendor and glory and yet so approachable - Your arms of love are open wide! I can feel You now! I tremble at Your touch! My heart beats wildly for You. I'm the one You love! Glory! Hallelujah! I'm loved! I belong! I belong to You! I'm Yours and You are mine, and Your banner over me is love, love, love! My dreams are fulfilled in You as I walk out the destiny You have for me. Great, exciting and enthralling is my future with You, my Bridegroom King. YOU are my VISION. You are all I want! Draw me deeper in You, and let us run together in anointed ministry!

Bridegroom: Yes, you, My Bride, are My beautiful rose and the song I sing! You are My delightful and glorious inheritance from My Father. You are My treasured possession. Joy floods My heart as I see you receiving the revelation of who you are! I chose you in love forever, before the earth was ever created! I cherish you and carry you as the Valentine of My heart! I invite you to be Mine, for I am yours, always and forever!

Scripture Reading: SS 2:1-7 (tPt); Eph. 1:4,18; John 8:32; Deut. 26:18

Encounter the Bridegroom God

Encounter the Bridegroom King as you read today's devotion (see Simple Steps to Encountering God and Sample Outline in Introduction). Continue your encounter with the Lord in your safe place. Journal as you share your hearts with one another.

Safe Place (describe)

_____
_____
_____

Thank You, Father, for giving me my identity. Can You tell me again who I am?

_____
_____
_____
_____
_____
_____
_____
_____
_____

Jesus, how do I delight You?

_____
_____
_____
_____

Bridegroom King, how do You want to celebrate me?

_____
_____
_____
_____

Thank You that You are singing over me with joy. Thank You that I am Your treasured possession. Thank You for...

_____
_____
_____

What truths are the Bridegroom/Papa/Holy Spirit speaking over you today? Write down these truths and speak them out loud as you see these truths in your imagination (i.e. He calls you beautiful, so see yourself as beautiful as you say out loud, "I'm beautiful!").

_____
_____
_____
_____
_____
_____
_____

What lies have you been believing? Ask the Lord to set you free from any deception and then focus on the Lord and His truth. Agree with God, and declare His life over you, as you speak/sing His truth.

_____
_____
_____
_____
_____
_____

How does the Bridegroom God feel about you? See you?

_____
_____
_____
_____
_____
_____
_____

Who do you say the Lord is? (Matt. 16:13) Who you believe God to be will affect every area of your walk with Him. Speak the truth and see it!

_____
_____
_____
_____
_____
_____

Who does the Lord say you are? What's the truth about your identity and your destiny? What you believe about yourself will affect every area of your walk with Him. Speak the truth out loud and see it.

_____
_____
_____
_____
_____
_____
_____
_____

How has the Lord shown you His extravagant love and how has He kissed you today?

_____
_____
_____
_____
_____
_____
_____
_____
_____

Worship Him and thank Him for Who he is!

_____
_____
_____
_____
_____
_____
_____
_____
_____
_____
_____
_____
_____

Arise, My Bride, and walk in your destiny! It's a new beginning!

Day 8

"Sustain me with cakes of raisins, refresh me with apples, for I am lovesick..."
SS 2:5 (NKJV)

Bride: Revive me, refresh me and renew me! Sustain and strengthen me to never quit or give up. Revive me with a drink of Your glory and unconditional love! Refresh me with Your Word! Renew me with Your very fires of passion and affection that overwhelm me! Wash over me with Your glorious river of peace and joy! Remind me of and reenergize me once again with the promises in Your Word that bring me new life. I'm crying out for help! I am hungry and thirsty for more. Thank You that there is always more in You! I am longing for more and so lovesick for You, my Beautiful King! I am desperate for more, yet at the same time, at rest in Your glorious love! This must be heaven on earth!

Bridegroom: My Beauty, fall into My arms of love and rest next to My heart. Let Me revive, refresh and renew you as you put your head on My shoulder. I am able to carry every burden you have. Let Me sustain and strengthen you to never give up and to endure to the end. Do you know the joy I have in My heart for you? Seeing this joy that I have over you is the very thing that will strengthen and energize you to fulfill your destiny. The joy of the Lord over you is your strength! Look for My joy! Come to Me when you are weary, and I will give you rest in My love. Come to Me and receive My precious promises. Come to Me and drink, and a river of life will continually flow from within you to bring peace, joy and love to you and to everyone you come in contact with. Come to Me and be reawakened, recharged and rekindled. I am your King of Glory. Come and drink of My glory and be restored! My arms are open wide!

Scripture Reading: SS 2:1-7 (NKJV); Neh. 8:10; Matt.11:28; John 7:37-39

Encounter the Bridegroom God

Encounter the Bridegroom King as you read today's devotion (see Simple Steps to Encountering God and Sample Outline in Introduction). Continue your encounter with the Lord in your safe place. Journal as you share your hearts with one another.

Safe Place (describe)

_____
_____
_____

Yeshua, am I carrying a burden that isn't mine? If so, what is it and how do I let go and give it to You?

_____
_____
_____
_____
_____

Bridegroom King, can you show me a picture of the joy that You have over me?

_____
_____
_____
_____
_____
_____

Jesus, what are the promises you have given me?

_____
_____
_____
_____
_____

Thank You, Yeshua, that Your joy over me is my strength! Thank You that You renew, refresh and revive me. Thank you for...

_____
_____
_____

What truths are the Bridegroom/Papa/Holy Spirit speaking over you today? Write down these truths and speak them out loud as you see these truths in your imagination (i.e. He calls you beautiful, so see yourself as beautiful as you say out loud, "I'm beautiful!").

_____
_____
_____
_____
_____
_____
_____

What lies have you been believing? Ask the Lord to set you free from any deception and then focus on the Lord and His truth. Agree with God, and declare His life over you, as you speak/sing His truth.

_____
_____
_____
_____
_____
_____
_____

How does the Bridegroom God feel about you? See you?

_____
_____
_____
_____
_____
_____
_____

Who do you say the Lord is? (Matt. 16:13) Who you believe God to be will affect every area of your walk with Him. Speak the truth and see it!

_____
_____
_____
_____
_____
_____

Who does the Lord say you are? What's the truth about your identity and your destiny? What you believe about yourself will affect every area of your walk with Him. Speak the truth out loud and see it.

_____

_____

_____

_____

_____

_____

_____

_____

_____

_____

_____

How has the Lord shown you His extravagant love and how has He kissed you today?

_____

_____

_____

_____

_____

_____

_____

_____

Worship Him and thank Him for Who He is!

_____

_____

_____

_____

_____

_____

_____

_____

Arise, My Bride, and walk in your destiny! It's a fresh start!

Day 9

"The one I love calls to me:" SS 2:10 (tPt)

Bride: My Beloved calls to me. At the sound of His voice, my heart boils over with passion for Him. My glorious King comes to me no matter where I am. Even when I'm in the shadows hiding, He comes and He finds me. His love is unrelenting. His love never fails. He never gives up on me! Never! He loves me! He loves me! He loves me!

Bridegroom: Rise up, My Love, My Beautiful One, and come with Me! Let us run to the higher places! There are exciting adventures ahead for us together! Say, "Yes," my Bride! Now is the time! It's a new season, a new day and a new beginning! Winter has finally come to an end, and your time of hiding is over! Come out, my Bride, and arise! Come out from the shadows! Come out from the fear and anxiety. Come out from the shame and condemnation. Come out, come out, wherever you are, and run with Me! My Love, My blood has set you free to walk in the light of My glory and to unlock the prison doors of fear, shame and condemnation for many. We have had such sweet communion in the garden together and your love has grown beyond your fears, for My perfect love casts out all fear. I love you, I love you, I love you! Trust Me, My Precious One. Continue to receive My love within and allow all fear, even the tiny traces of fear, to be driven out. I'll do My part, and you do your part. Together we will be more than conquerors on the mountains of warfare! Together we will set you free! Together we will set the captives free, bringing healing and the love of My Father to the world! Say, "Yes," My Darling, say, "Yes!"

Scriptures Reading: SS 2:8-10 (tPt); I John 4:19; Rom. 8:37; I Cor. 13:8

Encounter the Bridegroom God

Encounter the Bridegroom King as you read today's devotion (see Simple Steps to Encountering God and Sample Outline in Introduction). Continue your encounter with the Lord in your safe place. Journal as you share your hearts with one another.

Safe Place (describe)

_____
_____
_____

Jesus, what shadow am I hiding behind?

_____
_____
_____
_____
_____
_____

Yeshua, would you come and bring me out from the darkness and into your marvelous light?

_____
_____
_____
_____
_____

How do you want to set me free?

_____
_____
_____
_____
_____

Thank you so much for coming to me wherever I am! Thank You for bringing me out of the shadows! Thank You for Your perfect love that drives out all fear. Thank You for...

_____
_____
_____

What truths are the Bridegroom/Papa/Holy Spirit speaking over you today? Write down these truths and speak them out loud as you see these truths in your imagination (i.e. He calls you beautiful, so see yourself as beautiful as you say out loud, "I'm beautiful!").

_____

_____

_____

_____

_____

_____

_____

What lies have you been believing? Ask the Lord to set you free from any deception and then focus on the Lord and His truth. Agree with God, and declare His life over you, as you speak/sing His truth.

_____

_____

_____

_____

_____

_____

How does the Bridegroom God feel about you? See you?

_____

_____

_____

_____

_____

_____

_____

Who do you say the Lord is? (Matt. 16:13) Who you believe God to be will affect every area of your walk with Him. Speak the truth and see it!

_____

_____

_____

_____

_____

_____

_____

Who does the Lord say you are? What's the truth about your identity and your destiny? What you believe about yourself will affect every area of your walk with Him. Speak the truth out loud and see it.

_____
_____
_____
_____
_____
_____
_____
_____
_____
_____
_____

How has the Lord shown you His extravagant love and how has He kissed you today?

_____
_____
_____
_____
_____
_____
_____
_____
_____

Worship Him and thank Him for Who He is!

_____
_____
_____
_____
_____
_____
_____
_____
_____
_____

Arise, My Bride, and walk in your destiny! It's a new day!

Day 10

Arise, my darling, my beautiful one, and come with me." SS 2:10 (NIV)

Bridegroom: Come with Me, My Dearest Darling, My Beautiful One! Rise up and be awakened by the kisses of My heart, the kisses of My affectionate love, the kisses of heaven! For now is the time to arise and come deeper into My heart as you open wide the door of your heart and invite Me in! Come with Me to the deepest places of love. Come with Me into the intimate glory chambers of My heart and know Me - you in Me and Me in you. Trust in Me with all your heart and lean not on your own understanding and come. This is eternal life, that you may know Me, by intimately feeling and perceiving my presence. I'm jealous for you, for all of you. I love you and yearn for you. Come...

Bride: I know You are my Lover and I am Yours, for I delight in You and You delight in Me, as we share our hearts together. You mean everything to me for You are my life and my First Love. I open wide the doors of my heart and welcome You in to every area of my heart. I hold nothing back from You, for You have held nothing back from me. Arise, my Beautiful Bridegroom King, and take over my heart. Sit on the throne of my heart as true King and Lover. I ask for Your Spirit of wisdom and revelation so that I would know Your heart intimately. I want to know You, Jesus, and the power of Your resurrection and the fellowship of sharing in Your sufferings. I am Yours completely, and You are mine totally. We delight ourselves in each other from dusk to dawn and from dawn to dusk. I don't want to live a moment without You.

Scripture Reading: SS 2:10-13 (NIV); Rev. 3:20; James 4:5; John 17:3; Phil. 3:10; Eph. 1:17

Encounter the Bridegroom God

Encounter the Bridegroom King as you read today's devotion (see Simple Steps to Encountering God and Sample Outline in Introduction). Continue your encounter with the Lord in your safe place. Journal as you share your hearts with one another.

Safe Place (describe)

_____

_____

_____

Yeshua, what part of my heart do you want to possess that I have kept control over?

_____

_____

_____

What is keeping me from trusting you with that part of my heart?

_____

_____

_____

_____

_____

_____

Lord, would you prove your love to that part of my heart?

_____

_____

_____

_____

_____

_____

Thank You, Jesus, for loving all of me. Thank you for inviting me to come deeper into your heart. Thank You that I can trust You. Thank You for...

_____

_____

_____

_____

What truths are the Bridegroom/Papa/Holy Spirit speaking over you today? Write down these truths and speak them out loud as you see these truths in your imagination (i.e. He calls you beautiful, so see yourself as beautiful as you say out loud, "I'm beautiful!").

_____
_____
_____
_____
_____
_____
_____

What lies have you been believing? Ask the Lord to set you free from any deception and then focus on the Lord and His truth. Agree with God, and declare His life over you, as you speak/sing His truth.

_____
_____
_____
_____
_____
_____

How does the Bridegroom God feel about you? See you?

_____
_____
_____
_____
_____
_____
_____

Who do you say the Lord is? (Matt. 16:13) Who you believe God to be will affect every area of your walk with Him. Speak the truth and see it!

_____
_____
_____
_____
_____
_____
_____

Who does the Lord say you are? What's the truth about your identity and your destiny? What you believe about yourself will affect every area of your walk with Him. Speak the truth out loud and see it.

_____
_____
_____
_____
_____
_____
_____
_____
_____
_____
_____
_____

How has the Lord shown you His extravagant love and how has He kissed you today?

_____
_____
_____
_____
_____
_____
_____
_____
_____

Worship Him and thank Him for Who He is!

_____
_____
_____
_____
_____
_____
_____
_____
_____

Arise, My Bride, and walk in your destiny! It's a new day!

Day 11

"Can you not discern this new day of destiny breaking forth around you? The early signs of my purposes and plans are bursting forth." SS 2:13 (tPt)

Bridegroom: Arise, My Darling! Awaken to a new day dawning! It's a new season full of fruitful destiny breaking forth all around you! Doors of revelation and relationship are wide open, and I'm inviting you to walk through those doors into the cloud-filled chambers of glory in My heart! It's a season of deeper intimacy, deeper love and greater power! Come up higher! I want you to be in the middle of all I'm doing in this hour of history. It's the greatest time for you to be alive! I have an astonishing plan and purpose for you, a life of abundance in Me! The enemy is out to steal, kill and destroy your identity and your destiny. But I have come to destroy the works of the enemy and to bring you the victory as you partner with Me! I chose you! You need not fear! You are My joy and My song! I'm singing over you even now. Can you hear it? I bless you, My Beauty, to know you are loved and to flow in My authority! I am the most joyful man in history! You are the joy set before Me, and I can't help dancing and singing for joy over you. I am so joyful about YOU and so glad to be with YOU! I love you and I'm calling you to arise in this new day! Arise now, into your destiny!

Bride: You are my Song of all Songs! I hear you singing with joy and see You dancing over me with great delight! What ecstasy fills my heart! You are joyful about me! You really love me, and You really like me! You have a plan for my life! I have purpose and destiny in You, Lord! Amazing! You are everything I've ever needed and everything I've ever longed for. Yeshua, I love you!

Scripture Reading: SS 2:13 (tPt); Heb. 12:2; Zeph. 3:17; John 10:10; I John 3:8

Encounter the Bridegroom God

Encounter the Bridegroom King as you read today's devotional (see Simple Steps to Encountering God and Sample Outline in Introduction). Continue your encounter with the Lord in your safe place. Journal as you share your hearts with one another.

Safe Place (describe)

_____
_____
_____

Lord, can You give me a picture of Your joy and delight over me?

_____
_____
_____

Jesus, what is the love song You are singing over me now?

_____
_____

Lord, why is this the greatest time for me to be alive?

_____
_____
_____

Bridegroom King, how do you want to partner with me in the earth?

_____
_____
_____
_____

What does it mean that you not only love me but that you like me?

_____
_____
_____

Thank You, Bridegroom King, for Your joy and gladness over me. Thank You that I have purpose and destiny in You. Thank You for...

_____
_____

What truths are the Bridegroom/Papa/Holy Spirit speaking over you today? Write down these truths and speak them out loud as you see these truths in your imagination (i.e. He calls you beautiful, so see yourself as beautiful as you say out loud, "I'm beautiful!").

_____
_____
_____
_____
_____
_____
_____

What lies have you been believing? Ask the Lord to set you free from any deception and then focus on the Lord and His truth. Agree with God, and declare His life over you, as you speak/sing His truth.

_____
_____
_____
_____
_____
_____
_____

How does the Bridegroom God feel about you? See you?

_____
_____
_____
_____
_____
_____
_____

Who do you say the Lord is? (Matt. 16:13) Who you believe God to be will affect every area of your walk with Him. Speak the truth and see it!

_____
_____
_____
_____
_____
_____
_____

Who does the Lord say you are? What's the truth about your identity and your destiny? What you believe about yourself will affect every area of your walk with Him. Speak the truth out loud and see it.

_____
_____
_____
_____
_____
_____
_____
_____
_____
_____

How has the Lord shown you His extravagant love and how has He kissed you today?

_____
_____
_____
_____
_____
_____
_____
_____

Worship Him and thank Him for Who He is!

_____
_____
_____
_____
_____
_____
_____
_____
_____

Arise, My Bride, and walk in your destiny! It's a new season!

Day 12

"...show me your face, let me hear your voice; for your voice is sweet and your face is lovely." SS 2:14b (NIV)

Bridegroom: Oh, My Darling, I long to see your radiant face and hear your beautiful voice. Your face shines so brightly, and your voice is delicious to Me! Your face glows with passion for Me, and your voice is anointed with grace as you speak words of beauty, glory and life to Me. You have heard My love song over you, and I long to hear you singing your love song over Me. Come closer, my Love, and turn your face and your voice toward Me. You are beautiful! And I love you!

Bride: Oh, my Bridegroom King! How passionately my heart burns for you! You see my face as lovely and radiant! You want to hear my whispers of longing. You enjoy hearing my songs of love and worship over You. Here I come, running into Your arms of love! My heart is undone! I can't help but worship You! I will worship You forever! You are worthy, My King, to receive glory and honor and power, for you created it all because you wanted it. You created me and planned for me because you wanted me! Thank You for wanting me and thank you for giving me life! I will let You see my face for I long for face-to-face communion with You! I will let you hear my voice in song and prayer! I will join You, Jesus, the greatest Intercessor of all time, in prayer and intercession as you teach me and lead me. I will worship and praise Your Name, Yeshua, forever and ever for Yours is the Kingdom and the power and the glory forever! Amen!

Scriptures Reading: SS 2:14 (tPt); Ps. 9:1-2, 63:1-8, 98:1; Rev. 4:11; Matt. 6:13 (NKJV)

Encounter the Bridegroom God

Encounter the Bridegroom King as you read today's devotional (see Simple Steps to Encountering God and Sample Outline in Introduction). Continue your encounter with the Lord in your safe place. Journal as you share your hearts with one another.

Safe Place (describe)

_____
_____
_____

Bridegroom King, can You show me how my face is lovely to You?

_____
_____
_____
_____

Jesus, can you help me to see myself as You see me?

_____
_____
_____
_____

Lord, in what ways do you appreciate hearing my voice?

_____
_____
_____

May I sing over you, Bridegroom King? Would you fill my mouth with all You are and all that You have done for me?

_____
_____
_____
_____

Thank You, Bridegroom King, for Your love for me. Thank You that You created me because You want me. Thank You for...

_____
_____
_____

What truths are the Bridegroom/Papa/Holy Spirit speaking over you today? Write down these truths and speak them out loud as you see these truths in your imagination (i.e. He calls you beautiful, so see yourself as beautiful as you say out loud, "I'm beautiful!").

_____

_____

_____

_____

_____

_____

_____

What lies have you been believing? Ask the Lord to set you free from any deception and then focus on the Lord and His truth. Agree with God, and declare His life over you, as you speak/sing His truth.

_____

_____

_____

_____

_____

_____

_____

How does the Bridegroom God feel about you? See you?

_____

_____

_____

_____

_____

_____

_____

Who do you say the Lord is? (Matt. 16:13) Who you believe God to be will affect every area of your walk with Him. Speak the truth and see it!

_____

_____

_____

_____

_____

_____

_____

Who does the Lord say you are? What's the truth about your identity and your destiny? What you believe about yourself will affect every area of your walk with Him. Speak the truth out loud and see it.

_____
_____
_____
_____
_____
_____
_____
_____
_____
_____
_____
_____

How has the Lord shown you His extravagant love and how has He kissed you today?

_____
_____
_____
_____
_____
_____
_____
_____
_____

Worship Him and thank Him for Who he is!

_____
_____
_____
_____
_____
_____
_____
_____
_____

Arise, My Bride, and walk in your destiny! It's a new day!

Day 13

"Catch for us the foxes, the little foxes that ruin the vineyards," SS 2:15 (NIV)

Bridegroom: My Dearest Darling, catch those sly, little foxes that are ruining your fruitfulness. Give to Me those troubling areas in your life that hinder our love relationship! Humble yourself and lay down at My feet those areas of compromise that are hidden deep in your heart. I will give you the victory over them, as you partner with Me in removing them. Don't allow fear to hold you back, but let My perfect LOVE win! Let the light of My love shine on those dark places that don't seem like that big of a deal to you, because in reality they are entangling you and holding you back from all that I've called you to. I love you, My Darling, and I want you to run FREE with Me on the mountaintops. I want you to run the race and win! I want you to win the prize for which I have called you heavenward in My Love.

Bride: Oh, My Darling, HELP! Help me to catch those little foxes that steal from my fruitfulness. I long to be victorious and to bear fruit in Your kingdom that lasts forever! I do agree with You and partner with You, Yeshua, to remove the dark areas of compromise. I agree with You, My Beloved, to allow Your healing love and light to flood me that I might fulfill my destiny in You. Knowing Your truth will set me free. You are Truth! Knowing You intimately will set me free! Fear has no place in my life, not even a trace of fear! For you didn't give me a spirit of fear, but a Spirit of power and of love and of a sound mind! I want You more than fear! Yeshua, come and drive out all fear in my life. I want to be free to receive Your love, love You back, love myself, and love all those You place in my path. I want to love You with a deeper intimacy, and I want to run with You in anointed ministry on the mountains. Search me, Jesus, and know my heart; try me, and know my fears and worries and see if there is any wicked way in me. Lead me in Your ways and in Your truth. In You, I am more than a conqueror because of Your great love. Together we will overcome the foxes!

Scripture Reading: SS 2:15 (tPt); Phil. 3:14; 2 Tim. 1:7; Ps. 139:23; I John 4:18

Encounter the Bridegroom God

Encounter the Bridegroom King as you read today's devotional (see Simple Steps to Encountering God and Sample Outline in Introduction). Continue your encounter with the Lord in your safe place. Journal as you share your hearts with one another.

Safe Place (describe)

_____

_____

_____

Lord, what are the foxes in my life that hinder my love relationship with you?

_____

_____

_____

Jesus, how do you want me to partner with you to overcome the foxes in my life?

_____

_____

_____

_____

_____

_____

What are the lies about the foxes that I believe? What is the truth about the foxes?

_____

_____

_____

_____

_____

Thank You, Yeshua, that together we are overcoming the foxes in my life. Thank, Lord, that I am more than a conqueror because of Your great love. Thank You for...

_____

_____

_____

What truths are the Bridegroom/Papa/Holy Spirit speaking over you today? Write down these truths and speak them out loud as you see these truths in your imagination (i.e. He calls you beautiful, so see yourself as beautiful as you say out loud, "I'm beautiful!").

_____

_____

_____

_____

_____

_____

_____

What lies have you been believing? Ask the Lord to set you free from any deception and then focus on the Lord and His truth. Agree with God, and declare His life over you, as you speak/sing His truth.

_____

_____

_____

_____

_____

_____

_____

How does the Bridegroom God feel about you? See you?

_____

_____

_____

_____

_____

_____

_____

Who do you say the Lord is? (Matt. 16:13) Who you believe God to be will affect every area of your walk with Him. Speak the truth and see it!

_____

_____

_____

_____

_____

_____

_____

Who does the Lord say you are? What's the truth about your identity and your destiny? What you believe about yourself will affect every area of your walk with Him. Speak the truth out loud and see it.

_____
_____
_____
_____
_____
_____
_____
_____
_____
_____

How has the Lord shown you His extravagant love and how has He kissed you today?

_____
_____
_____
_____
_____
_____
_____
_____

Worship and thank Him for Who He is!

_____
_____
_____
_____
_____
_____
_____
_____
_____

Arise, My Bride, in the joy of being loved and walk in your destiny!

Day 14

"My lover is mine and I am His,"

SS 2:16 (NIV)

Bride: You, my Beloved, are mine and I am Yours! You belong to me, and I belong to You! I know now where I belong! I belong with You! You are mine, and I am Yours. We belong to each other, and, even though I'm struggling right now with fear, I trust You, and know that You will never leave me or forsake me. Your arms of love are open wide, beckoning patiently for me to come. I long to come away with You, but there is a battle raging inside of me. Help me! I'm crying out for You! I need You. My Bridegroom Lover, come and set me free, driving out the enemy's grip of fear. I love You.

Bridegroom: I love you, Darling, and you are Mine. You have given yourself to Me in the light of the revelation that you have at this time. Your fears are great, but you know that I love you in spite of your weaknesses. I expected this. I knew you would not be mature when you first fell in love with Me. I knew that it would take time for you to progressively grow more like Me and let go of fear. Remember that I did not give you a spirit of fear, but a Spirit of power, and of love and of a sound mind. As you let My love flood you, fear will have to leave and you will be filled with my power to walk out the destiny I created you to fulfill. I saw you when you were formed in your mother's womb, and I know everything about you - the times of joy and the times of pain. AND I LOVE AND CHERISH YOU. You are Mine. You belong to Me. You are My Glorious Bride. You are beautiful beyond description. I love you, and I will never change My mind about you!

Scripture Reading: SS 2:16-17; Heb. 13:5b; 2 Tim. 1:7; Ps. 139:13

Encounter the Bridegroom God

Encounter the Bridegroom King as you read today's devotional (see Simple Steps to Encountering God and Sample Outline in Introduction). Continue your encounter with the Lord in your safe place. Journal as you share your hearts with one another.

Safe Place (describe)

_____
_____
_____

What fears do you want to free me from?

_____
_____
_____
_____

Jesus, how can I open my heart wider to receive more of Your love so that fear, anxiety and worry will have to leave?

_____
_____
_____

How can You know everything about me and still love me?

_____
_____
_____
_____

I've often felt left out, but You say I belong. Why?

_____
_____
_____
_____

Thank You, Yeshua, that You say I belong. Thank You that You know everything about me and You still love me! Thank You for...

_____
_____
_____

What truths are the Bridegroom/Papa/Holy Spirit speaking over you today? Write down these truths and speak them out loud as you see these truths in your imagination (i.e. He calls you beautiful, so see yourself as beautiful as you say out loud, "I'm beautiful!").

_____
_____
_____
_____
_____
_____
_____

What lies have you been believing? Ask the Lord to set you free from any deception and then focus on the Lord and His truth. Agree with God, and declare His life over you, as you speak/sing His truth.

_____
_____
_____
_____
_____
_____
_____

How does the Bridegroom God feel about you? See you?

_____
_____
_____
_____
_____
_____
_____

Who do you say the Lord is? (Matt. 16:13) Who you believe God to be will affect every area of your walk with Him. Speak the truth and see it!

_____
_____
_____
_____
_____
_____
_____

Who does the Lord say you are? What's the truth about your identity and your destiny? What you believe about yourself will affect every area of your walk with Him. Speak the truth out loud and see it.

_____
_____
_____
_____
_____
_____
_____
_____
_____
_____
_____

How has the Lord shown you His extravagant love and how has He kissed you today?

_____
_____
_____
_____
_____
_____
_____
_____
_____
_____

Worship and thank Him for Who He is!

_____
_____
_____
_____
_____
_____
_____
_____

Arise, My Bride, and walk in your destiny! It's a new day!

Day 15

"Night after night I'm tossing and turning...Why did I let him go from me? How my heart now aches for him...So I must rise in search of him...nothing will keep me from my search..." SS 3:1 (tPt)

Bride: I longed and ached to go with You, my Beloved, but fear stopped me. Why did I not obey? Life without feeling Your presence and anointing is far more miserable than anything that could have happened to me had I obeyed. I will search for You, Yeshua, the One I love - the One I must have, for I cannot live without You! I'm desperate! I know You are still here with me, even though I cannot feel You, but I cannot live life like this! I must obey You and find Your affirming manifest presence. I cannot go on without Your glory and Your light. I will search for You until I find You and feel Your presence with me once again!

Bridegroom: My Darling, I have never left you and never will! I love YOU forever and always and My love for you will never change! I lifted My manifest presence from you because you would not obey Me. I know that you did not refuse to obey because of rebellion in your heart. You disobeyed because of immaturity and fear! But I cannot allow you to stay there! I have lifted My manifest presence from you to pry your fingers off the comfort zone you want to remain in. When you let go, you will grow up and mature in Me! I love you too much to leave you where you are spiritually! I love you, and I call you and draw you up higher, My Sweetheart. My heart aches for you to come running back into My arms of love. Die to yourself and come! Focus on Me! Keep your eyes and gaze set on Me and lay aside the sin that so easily entangles you. When you search for Me, you will find Me, when you seek Me with all your heart.

Scripture Reading: SS 3:1-4 (tPt); John 14:15; Heb. 12:1; Jer. 29:13

Encounter the Bridegroom God

Encounter the Bridegroom King as you read today's devotional (see Simple Steps to Encountering God and Sample Outline in Introduction). Continue your encounter with the Lord in your safe place. Journal as you share your hearts with one another.

Safe Place (describe)

_____

_____

_____

Lord, am I hanging on to my comfort zone right now?

_____

_____

_____

Bridegroom King, how have I settled for comfort and second best instead of rising up in obedience to You?

_____

_____

_____

_____

Yeshua, how do you want to set this captive free from the ease of comfort?

_____

_____

_____

_____

Jesus, would you show me again how much you love me even in my struggle?

_____

_____

_____

Thank You, Yeshua, that Your love for me never changes! Thank You that You love me always and forever! Thank You for...

_____

_____

What truths are the Bridegroom/Papa/Holy Spirit speaking over you today? Write down these truths and speak them out loud as you see these truths in your imagination (i.e. He calls you beautiful, so see yourself as beautiful as you say out loud, "I'm beautiful!").

_____
_____
_____
_____
_____
_____
_____

What lies have you been believing? Ask the Lord to set you free from any deception and then focus on the Lord and His truth. Agree with God, and declare His life over you, as you speak/sing His truth.

_____
_____
_____
_____
_____
_____

How does the Bridegroom God feel about you? See you?

_____
_____
_____
_____
_____
_____
_____

Who do you say the Lord is? (Matt. 16:13) Who you believe God to be will affect every area of your walk with Him. Speak the truth and see it!

_____
_____
_____
_____
_____
_____

Who does the Lord say you are? What's the truth about your identity and your destiny? What you believe about yourself will affect every area of your walk with Him. Speak the truth out loud and see it.

_____
_____
_____
_____
_____
_____
_____
_____

How has the Lord shown you His extravagant love and how has He kissed you today?

_____
_____
_____
_____
_____
_____
_____
_____
_____
_____
_____
_____
_____
_____

Worship Him and thank Him for Who He is!

_____
_____
_____
_____
_____
_____
_____
_____

Arise, My Bride, in my love and walk in your destiny! It's a new day!

Day 16

"...I found the one my heart loves."
SS 3:4 (NIV)

Bride: I became desperate for You, my Beloved, and I found You! I got up, obeyed You, and encountered You! I did not give up! You stirred up my hunger and thirst to come after You! I would not quit asking, seeking and knocking for more of You until I found You. You withdrew Your manifest presence that my heart would burn with fiery passionate love for You...so much so that I would obey You! I cannot live without You! I must have MORE of You, My Bridegroom King! I ask that You would continue to help me to delight in the proper Fear of the Lord as You did! I want to delight in fearing and being in awe of You so that I would never hurt You or disobey You. I long for a deeper intimacy with You! Deep calls to deep! I'm desperate! I'm empowered by Your love to love You back and to obey You! I long to worship You face to face! I desire to walk in obedience to You, My Lord. My heart burns for You!

Bridegroom: Your hunger and thirst and desperation are a beautiful thing to Me! Your willingness to be obedient is beautiful! You would not give up or quit! You decided in your heart that you would not live life without My presence and glory and that you would obey! You decided that you would never give up until you found Me again in a deeper way. Yes, the Spirit of the Fear of the Lord was My delight and it shall be your delight as well, as you receive the depths of My love for you. Delighting in the Spirit of the Fear of the Lord only takes you deeper in My love and intimacy for it acknowledges that I am light and in Me is no darkness at all, only good. Delighting in the Fear of the Lord brings obedience, where Your desire is not your own will, but the will of My Father. When you delight in the Fear of the Lord, your heart is tender towards Me and you experience revival. You never want to hurt Me. You only want to please Me and love Me more. Proper fear of Me is true love. Your love and worship are beautiful to Me. You bring great joy and gladness to My heart! You shall have your desire!
Scripture Reading: SS 3:4-11(tPt); Matt. 7:7-8; Is. 11:3; John 14:15, 23; I John 1:5; Ps. 42:7

Encounter the Bridegroom God

Encounter the Bridegroom King as you read today's devotional (see Simple Steps to Encountering God and Sample Outline in Introduction). Continue your encounter with the Lord in your safe place. Journal as you share your hearts with one another.

Safe Place (describe)

_____
_____
_____

Lord, would you continue to cause the fire to burn in my heart for You?

_____
_____
_____

Jesus, how can I embrace the true Spirit of the Fear of the Lord and delight in it? Do I need to be afraid?

_____
_____
_____
_____
_____
_____

Yeshua, what are the benefits of truly delighting in the Spirit of the Fear of the Lord?

_____
_____
_____
_____
_____

Thank You, Father, that you are light and that You always are good! Thank You that You always have my best in mind! Thank You for...

_____
_____
_____
_____

What truths are the Bridegroom/Papa/Holy Spirit speaking over you today? Write down these truths and speak them out loud as you see these truths in your imagination (i.e. He calls you beautiful, so see yourself as beautiful as you say out loud, "I'm beautiful!").

_____

_____

_____

_____

_____

_____

_____

What lies have you been believing? Ask the Lord to set you free from any deception and then focus on the Lord and His truth. Agree with God, and declare His life over you, as you speak/sing His truth.

_____

_____

_____

_____

_____

_____

_____

How does the Bridegroom God feel about you? See you?

_____

_____

_____

_____

_____

_____

_____

Who do you say the Lord is? (Matt. 16:13) Who you believe God to be will affect every area of your walk with Him. Speak the truth and see it!

_____

_____

_____

_____

_____

_____

_____

Who does the Lord say you are? What's the truth about your identity and your destiny? What you believe about yourself will affect every area of your walk with Him. Speak the truth out loud and see it.

_____

_____

_____

_____

_____

_____

_____

How has the Lord shown you His extravagant love and how has He kissed you today?

_____

_____

_____

_____

_____

_____

_____

_____

Worship and thank Him for Who He is!

_____

_____

_____

_____

_____

_____

_____

_____

_____

_____

_____

_____

Awaken, My Bride, to my love and walk in your destiny! It's a new day!

Day 17

"Listen, my dearest darling, you are so beautiful - you are beauty itself to me! Your eyes glisten with love, like gentle doves behind your veil. What devotion I see each time I gaze upon you..." SS 4:1 (tPt)

Bridegroom: Listen, My Darling! Listen to the love song I am singing over you! You are beautiful, My Dove! You have eyes only for me! You are not distracted by the world. Your heart is so hungry and thirsty for Me and my righteousness. You shall be filled to overflowing! You are desperate for more! Your fiery heart of passion burns even brighter for Me and causes My heart to pound. Tears well up in your eyes as you gaze into Mine - seeing in my eyes of love the truth of who you really are. Your face glows with a glorious and holy splendor. I'm drawn by your beauty, inside and out! My delight is in you! I love you, My Dove!

Bride: Oh, My Bridegroom King, You have seen and know the fear that has been in my heart, and yet You still see me as Your Darling, Your Dove! I can't help but love You when I know You see me as I really am and yet You love me and call me Your Darling! All my imperfections don't worry You. Your tender affectionate love flows towards me through Your gaze, through Your voice and through Your touch! You are real! You see my devotion for You and say that I have eyes only for You. You see my weak love for you and say that it's real. You WOW me! Your eyes of revelation amaze me as You look at me prophetically and see me as I will become! Over and over, I keep falling deeper and deeper in love with You as I see how You love me! And the things that hinder my love for You are falling away! Your love is setting me free from sin! I'm overwhelmed with Your extravagant love, Yeshua, for you have brought me out of darkness into Your marvelous light! Whom have I in heaven but you, My Bridegroom King, and earth has nothing I desire besides you.

Scripture Reading: SS 4:1-5; Ps. 73:25; Matt. 5:6; I Peter 2:9

Encounter the Bridegroom God

Encounter the Bridegroom King as you read today's devotional (see Simple Steps to Encountering God and Sample Outline in Introduction). Continue your encounter with the Lord in your safe place. Journal as you share your hearts with one another.

Safe Place (describe)

_____
_____
_____

Lord, can You give me a picture of how beautiful I am to you?

_____
_____
_____

Bridegroom King, would you tell me again who I am?

_____
_____
_____
_____
_____
_____

Yeshua, thank you for seeing me as I will become. What do you see me becoming as you look at me prophetically?

_____
_____
_____
_____
_____
_____
_____

Thank You, Yeshua, that you have brought me out of darkness into Your marvelous light. Thank You for Your outrageous and extravagant love. Thank You for...

_____
_____
_____

What truths are the Bridegroom/Papa/Holy Spirit speaking over you today? Write down these truths and speak them out loud as you see these truths in your imagination (i.e. He calls you beautiful, so see yourself as beautiful as you say out loud, "I'm beautiful!").

_____

_____

_____

_____

_____

_____

_____

What lies have you been believing? Ask the Lord to set you free from any deception and then focus on the Lord and His truth. Agree with God, and declare His life over you, as you speak/sing His truth.

_____

_____

_____

_____

_____

_____

_____

How does the Bridegroom God feel about you? See you?

_____

_____

_____

_____

_____

_____

_____

Who do you say the Lord is? (Matt. 16:13) Who you believe God to be will affect every area of your walk with Him. Speak the truth and see it!

_____

_____

_____

_____

_____

_____

_____

Who does the Lord say you are? What's the truth about your identity and your destiny? What you believe about yourself will affect every area of your walk with Him. Speak the truth out loud and see it.

_____
_____
_____
_____
_____
_____
_____
_____
_____
_____
_____

How has the Lord shown you His extravagant love and how has He kissed you today?

_____
_____
_____
_____
_____
_____
_____
_____
_____

Worship and thank Him for Who He is!

_____
_____
_____
_____
_____
_____
_____
_____
_____
_____

Arise, My Bride, and experience the joy of being loved!!

Day 18

"Listen, my dearest darling, you are so beautiful - you are beauty itself to me."
SS 4:1 (tPt)

Bridegroom: Oh, My Bride, you are so beautiful! You have no idea how beautiful you are to Me. I see you, and I know all about you! I see your beautiful heart, and I see the darkness that's there, and yet, I choose to focus on the beauty within you because I know that you are in process! I see your humble heart and your agreement with Me about the darkness in your soul. I choose to see you prophetically - as you are becoming. I see with perfect eyes of revelation and prophesy those things that are not as though they were. I'm calling forth your beauty, your identity, your authority, and your destiny. When you fall, repent, hit delete, get up, and run back to Me. My arms of love are always open for you. When you fall, I am the One you need, so don't run away from Me. Come and fall on My love and mercy! Live like you are extravagantly loved all the days of your life. And love Me back extravagantly! You are beautiful beyond compare, My Beauty! There is none like you - not one! I'm for you and not against you. I love you with all My heart!

Bride: Oh, my beautiful Bridegroom King, Your pure, unconditional love and Your beauty take my breath away. Could this really be true? Could this really be happening to me? Could it be that I'm loved by the King of the universe in spite of my faults and sins? You still want me, and You still love me! I'm Yours my King! I know You love me right now, right where I'm at, and I can't help but love You with all my heart, all my soul and all my mind! Thank You that You love me and help me to continue to grow more like You. Thank You that You don't leave me where I'm at, but that you draw me with Your kindness and love! I'm lovesick for You, My Bridegroom. I cherish You with all my heart!

Scripture Reading: SS 4:1-5 (tPt); Rom. 4:17; 8:31; Matt. 22:37; Jer. 31:3

Encounter the Bridegroom God

Encounter the Bridegroom King as you read today's devotion (see Simple Steps to Encountering God and Sample Outline in Introduction). Continue your encounter with the Lord in your safe place. Journal as you share your hearts with one another.

Safe Place (describe)

_____
_____
_____

Lord, in spite of all my sins and weaknesses, I still say "Yes" and want You. Bridegroom King, do you still want me?

_____
_____
_____

Jesus, do you still love me right where I am, in spite of my faults?

_____
_____
_____

Holy Spirit, would You remind me not to waste time by beating myself up next time I blow it? Would you remind me to run right back into my Beloved's arms? Jesus, are Your arms open for me even when I sin?

_____
_____
_____
_____
_____
_____
_____
_____

Thank You, Yeshua, that You love me and are helping me to continue to grow more like You. Thank You for drawing me with Your lovingkindness. Thank You for...

_____
_____

What truths are the Bridegroom/Papa/Holy Spirit speaking over you today? Write down these truths and speak them out loud as you see these truths in your imagination (i.e. He calls you beautiful, so see yourself as beautiful as you say out loud, "I'm beautiful!").

_____
_____
_____
_____
_____
_____
_____

What lies have you been believing? Ask the Lord to set you free from any deception and then focus on the Lord and His truth. Agree with God, and declare His life over you, as you speak/sing His truth.

_____
_____
_____
_____
_____
_____

How does the Bridegroom God feel about you? See you?

_____
_____
_____
_____
_____
_____
_____

Who do you say the Lord is? (Matt. 16:13) Who you believe God to be will affect every area of your walk with Him. Speak the truth and see it!

_____
_____
_____
_____
_____
_____
_____

Who does the Lord say you are? What's the truth about your identity and your destiny? What you believe about yourself will affect every area of your walk with Him. Speak the truth out loud and see it.

_____
_____
_____
_____
_____
_____
_____
_____
_____
_____
_____

How has the Lord shown you His extravagant love and how has He kissed you today?

_____
_____
_____
_____
_____
_____
_____
_____
_____

Worship and thank Him for Who He is!

_____
_____
_____
_____
_____
_____
_____
_____
_____

Arise, My Bride, and walk in your destiny! It's a new day!

Day 19

"Until the day breaks and the shadows flee, I will go to the mountain of myrrh and to the hill of incense." SS 4:6 (NIV)

Bride: I've never experienced anything like this before. You never criticize me! You always speak the truth in love! You are always loving and kind, calling me higher and seeing me as I will become! There is absolutely nothing like knowing you are cherished and truly loved! I feel enjoyed, safe and absolutely beautiful! Because You are my safe Savior, my healing Love and constant Companion, I feel like I am more than a conqueror! Your extravagant love for me has transformed my life and given me the ability to overcome the fear in my heart, setting me free to leave the comfort zone. With You at my side, fear no longer has the same grip on my heart that it once did. You're in love with me and I'm in love with You. I feel loved and powerful and ready to go with You to the mountaintops!   My destiny in You is before me. We will minister together in Your love and power, seeing nations transformed as Your Kingdom comes on earth as it is in heaven. Together we will bind up the brokenhearted, proclaim freedom for the captives and release the prisoners from darkness. Many will be set free, saved, healed and filled with Your presence as we share Your amazing love. I can do all things through You, my King, Who strengthens me! With You all things are possible! I say, Yes! Yes, I will go with You no matter the cost! As I lean against You and hear Your heart beat for intercession, I agree with You, and embrace a life of abandoned worship and prayer. I will take up my cross and join You in the fellowship of sufferings, experiencing a deeper intimacy in You than I've ever known. Yes, my Love, I'm all in! Yes, I will go with You!

Bridegroom: You said, "Yes!" You have ravished My heart, My Beautiful Bride! Your "Yes" has stolen My heart! I am stunned by your flawless beauty! You have made my heart beat faster! I'm so thrilled that you want to run with Me, Darling, no matter the cost! I love you!

Scripture Reading: SS 4:6 (tPt); Phil 4:13; Prov. 28:1; Is. 61:1-3; Matt.19:26, 28:19

Encounter the Bridegroom God

Encounter the Bridegroom King as you read today's devotion (see Simple Steps to Encountering God and Sample Outline in Introduction). Continue your encounter with the Lord in your safe place. Journal as you share your hearts with one another.

Safe Place (describe)

_____
_____
_____

Bridegroom King, would you show me how to open up my heart and receive more of Your love so that I can love You more?

_____
_____
_____
_____

Lord, would you increase my capacity to receive more of Your love that Your love would overcome the fear that tries to keep me in the comfort zone?

_____
_____
_____

Jesus, would You help me to see the hurting and the wounded through Your eyes of compassion and love them with Your heart of love?

_____
_____
_____

Thank You, Jesus, for bringing healing to my heart. Thank You, Jesus, for loving me perfectly and always knowing what I need. Thank You for wanting to partner with me in ministry! Thank You for...

_____
_____
_____
_____
_____

What truths are the Bridegroom/Papa/Holy Spirit speaking over you today? Write down these truths and speak them out loud as you see these truths in your imagination (i.e. He calls you beautiful, so see yourself as beautiful as you say out loud, "I'm beautiful!").

_____
_____
_____
_____
_____
_____
_____

What lies have you been believing? Ask the Lord to set you free from any deception and then focus on the Lord and His truth. Agree with God, and declare His life over you, as you speak/sing His truth.

_____
_____
_____
_____
_____
_____
_____

How does the Bridegroom God feel about you? See you?

_____
_____
_____
_____
_____
_____
_____

Who do you say the Lord is? (Matt. 16:13) Who you believe God to be will affect every area of your walk with Him. Speak the truth and see it!

_____
_____
_____
_____
_____
_____
_____

Who does the Lord say you are? What's the truth about your identity and your destiny? What you believe about yourself will affect every area of your walk with Him. Speak the truth out loud and see it.

_____
_____
_____
_____
_____
_____
_____
_____
_____
_____
_____
_____

How has the Lord shown you His extravagant love and how has He kissed you today?

_____
_____
_____
_____
_____
_____
_____
_____
_____

Worship and thank Him for Who He is!

_____
_____
_____
_____
_____
_____
_____
_____
_____

Arise, My Bride, to the joy of being loved and walk in your destiny!

Day 20

"All beautiful you are, my darling; there is no flaw in you." SS 4:7 (NIV)

Bridegroom: You are altogether lovely and altogether beautiful, My Sweetheart! Because I have laid My life down for you at the cross and shed My blood for you, there is no flaw in you. Through My blood, I see you as perfect in every way. I see the "Yes," in your heart towards Me, and I'm undone! Do you know who you are? You are Mine! You are My Bride! You are loved! You are cherished and adored! You are beautiful! You are royalty! You are strong and mighty! You are priceless and precious! That's who you are! You are My beautiful Bride, and I see no spot or wrinkle in you. You are flawless. You are exquisite, a rare beauty!

Bride: Thank you for expressing to me the way You see me. I am undone and amazed that You look at me with such tender love and see through me to my beauty and my glory! Help me to see myself as You see me! It's only because of You, Yeshua, that You see me this way. You are the One who beautified me! It's only because of what You did for me at the cross that I'm altogether beautiful to You! It's only because of Your blood, which is Your perfect love, that You see no flaw in me! Thank You for Your love at the cross! Thank You that You paid it all! Thank You that You gave Your all! Thank You that You shed Your blood for me! I will take up my cross and follow You daily. I will never forget what You did for me! I will never forget Your love, Yeshua! Forever I will celebrate Your grace and Your mercy! I will always remember Your love for me at the cross! Thank You! You are worthy, worthy, worthy of my love and my all! You are beauty, beauty, beauty! You are glorious, glorious, glorious! You are holy, holy, holy, Lord God Almighty, Who was, Who is, and Who is to come! Thank You! Thank You! Thank You! I worship You! You are worthy! I must worship You! Your kingdom is a kingdom that will never end. To You, Jesus, be all glory and power and honor for ever and ever! Amen!

Scripture Reading: SS 4:7 (NIV); Luke 9:23; Rev. 1:5-6, 4:8b

Encounter the Bridegroom God

Encounter the Bridegroom King as you read today's devotion (see Simple Steps to Encountering God and Sample Outline in Introduction). Continue your encounter with the Lord in your safe place. Journal as you share your hearts with one another.

Safe Place (describe)

_____
_____
_____

Bridegroom King, would You tell me again who I am?

_____
_____
_____
_____
_____
_____

Papa, would You tell me again who I am?

_____
_____
_____
_____
_____
_____

Holy Spirit, would You tell me again who I am?

_____
_____
_____
_____
_____

Thank You that You see me without flaw and altogether beautiful! Thank You for beautifying me, Lord! Thank You for giving me my identity! Thank You for...

_____
_____

What truths are the Bridegroom/Papa/Holy Spirit speaking over you today? Write down these truths and speak them out loud as you see these truths in your imagination (i.e. He calls you beautiful, so see yourself as beautiful as you say out loud, "I'm beautiful!").

_____

_____

_____

_____

_____

_____

_____

What lies have you been believing? Ask the Lord to set you free from any deception and then focus on the Lord and His truth. Agree with God, and declare His life over you, as you speak/sing His truth.

_____

_____

_____

_____

_____

_____

_____

How does the Bridegroom God feel about you? See you?

_____

_____

_____

_____

_____

_____

_____

Who do you say the Lord is? (Matt. 16:13) Who you believe God to be will affect every area of your walk with Him. Speak the truth and see it!

_____

_____

_____

_____

_____

_____

_____

Who does the Lord say you are? What's the truth about your identity and your destiny? What you believe about yourself will affect every area of your walk with Him. Speak the truth out loud and see it.

_____

_____

_____

_____

_____

_____

_____

_____

_____

_____

How has the Lord shown you His extravagant love and how has He kissed you today?

_____

_____

_____

_____

_____

_____

_____

_____

_____

Worship Him and thank Him for Who He is!

_____

_____

_____

_____

_____

_____

_____

_____

_____

Arise, My Bride, and walk in your destiny! It's a new day!

Day 21

"Now you are ready, my bride, to come with me as we climb the highest peaks together." SS 4:8 (tPt)

Bridegroom: Oh, you are altogether lovely, altogether beautiful to Me, My cherished Bride! There is no flaw in you! Your "YES" has captured My heart! You are My radiant Beauty! I see you, through the blood I shed for you, as perfect, without stain or wrinkle. And now, you see yourself as I see you too, covered by My blood and loved, cherished, beautiful, pure, clean, lovely, unstoppable, powerful and fearless - a gorgeous Warrior Bride! Now you are ready, My Bride, to come with Me as we climb the highest mountain peaks together, warring against the enemy and his strategies. Now you are ready, My Bride, to come and fulfill your destiny by setting others free in My love. We will run on the mountaintops and roar in the heavens. Together we will preach My good news to the poor and comfort all who mourn. We will bestow on them a crown of beauty instead of ashes, the oil of joy instead of mourning and a garment of praise instead of a spirit of despair. We will lay hands on the sick and see them miraculously recover as My mighty power and love touches them. I'm thrilled that you want to run together! Out of our deep intimate love relationship, My authority and fruitfulness will flow through you to the nations.

Bride: Wow! You choose me to run with You on the mountaintops? I am chosen! I am chosen by the most beautiful Bridegroom, the most lavish Bridegroom, the ultimate Bridegroom of all time! I am thrilled and excited to partner with You, my Beautiful Bridegroom God! I am filled with greater longing and desire as I snuggle under the shadow of Your wing in the secret place of safety, and at the same time, know I will war and conquer with You on the mountaintops. I will dwell with You and gaze upon Your beauty all the days of my life! I will war with You, my King, as I rest in Your abundant, overflowing love! I will go with You wherever You lead, bringing hope to the world. Forever, I'm Yours!

Scripture Reading: SS 4:8 (tPt); Ps. 27:4, 91:1; Is. 61:1-3; Mark 16:18

Encounter the Bridegroom God

Encounter the Bridegroom King as you read today's devotion (see Simple Steps to Encountering God and Sample Outline in Introduction). Continue your encounter with the Lord in your safe place. Journal as you share your hearts with one another.

Safe Place (describe)

_____
_____
_____

Bridegroom King Jesus, am I ready to run with You in ministry? What does that look like?

_____
_____
_____
_____
_____

Jesus, will You walk with me as I love and care for the wounded and hurting?

_____
_____
_____
_____

Holy Spirit, would You touch others lives through me, anointing me to flow in the fruit and the gifts of the Spirit as well as in Your 7-fold Spirit?

_____
_____
_____
_____

Thank You, Bridegroom King, for drawing me into intimacy and running with me in anointed ministry. Thank You that out of our deep and intimate love relationship, authority and fruitfulness flow. Thank You for...

_____
_____
_____

What truths are the Bridegroom/Papa/Holy Spirit speaking over you today? Write down these truths and speak them out loud as you see these truths in your imagination (i.e. He calls you beautiful, so see yourself as beautiful as you say out loud, "I'm beautiful!").

_____
_____
_____
_____
_____
_____
_____

What lies have you been believing? Ask the Lord to set you free from any deception and then focus on the Lord and His truth. Agree with God, and declare His life over you, as you speak/sing His truth.

_____
_____
_____
_____
_____
_____
_____

How does the Bridegroom God feel about you? See you?

_____
_____
_____
_____
_____
_____
_____

Who do you say the Lord is? (Matt. 16:13) Who you believe God to be will affect every area of your walk with Him. Speak the truth and see it!

_____
_____
_____
_____
_____
_____
_____

Who does the Lord say you are? What's the truth about your identity and your destiny? What you believe about yourself will affect every area of your walk with Him. Speak the truth out loud and see it.

_____
_____
_____
_____
_____
_____
_____
_____
_____
_____
_____
_____

How has the Lord shown you His extravagant love and how has He kissed you today?

_____
_____
_____
_____
_____
_____
_____
_____
_____

Worship Him and thank Him for Who He is!

_____
_____
_____
_____
_____
_____
_____
_____
_____

Arise, My Bride, and walk in your destiny! It's a new day!

Day 22

"You have stolen my heart, my sister, my bride; you have stolen my heart with one glance of your eyes, with one jewel of your necklace." SS 4:9 (NIV)

Bridegroom: Oh, My Beauty! You have stolen My heart, My Sister, My Bride! You have stolen My heart with one glance of your eyes! My heart has been taken captive by your love! Just one glance My way, and I'm undone! Our love is intoxicating as our hearts beat together as one. You are My ravishing beauty! I can't take My eyes off of you! I will always cherish you! My heart beats wildly for you as you glance My way with one look of your eyes. Your beauty and your love have captured My heart, My Dearest. Nothing can separate us! I am convinced that neither death nor life, neither angels nor demons, neither the present nor the future, nor any powers, neither height nor depth, nor anything else in all creation, will be able to separate us from each other and from our Father's love! We are one, and My love conquers everything that comes against us! My love never fails! I am burning with Holy passion for you, My Precious One!

Bride: I love You! I love You! I love You, and my heart beats for You, my Prince of Peace, My Bridegroom God! One glance Your way and You say Your heart is captured! The revelation of Your love for me causes my heart to be captured as well, My King. My heart pounds passionately and yearns deeply for more of You! We are one! Nothing can separate us! Nothing in all creation can take me from You! We will be together forever! Your love has stolen my heart! I can't help falling in love with You again and again! I'm burning with holy, passionate, fiery love for You, Yeshua!

Scripture Reading: SS 4:9 (tPt); Rom. 8:38-39; I Cor. 13:8

Encounter the Bridegroom God

Encounter the Bridegroom King as you read today's devotion (see Simple Steps to Encountering God and Sample Outline in Introduction). Continue your encounter with the Lord in your safe place. Journal as you share your hearts with one another.

Safe Place (describe)

_____

_____

_____

How could You love me so much, Bridegroom God, that with just one glance of my eyes Your way, Your heart is undone?

_____

_____

_____

_____

_____

_____

How could weak, struggling me capture Your heart?

_____

_____

_____

What kind of a God are You that You would love me this way?

_____

_____

_____

Who am I, and who are You, that You would love me so extravagantly?

_____

_____

_____

Thank You, Bridegroom King for Your passionate fiery love for me. Thank You for touching the emotions of my heart and healing me deep within. Thank You for...

_____

_____

What truths are the Bridegroom/Papa/Holy Spirit speaking over you today? Write down these truths and speak them out loud as you see these truths in your imagination (i.e. He calls you beautiful, so see yourself as beautiful as you say out loud, "I'm beautiful!").

_____
_____
_____
_____
_____
_____
_____

What lies have you been believing? Ask the Lord to set you free from any deception and then focus on the Lord and His truth. Agree with God, and declare His life over you, as you speak/sing His truth.

_____
_____
_____
_____
_____
_____
_____

How does the Bridegroom God feel about you? See you?

_____
_____
_____
_____
_____
_____
_____

Who do you say the Lord is? (Matt. 16:13) Who you believe God to be will affect every area of your walk with Him. Speak the truth and see it!

_____
_____
_____
_____
_____
_____
_____

Who does the Lord say you are? What's the truth about your identity and your destiny? What you believe about yourself will affect every area of your walk with Him. Speak the truth out loud and see it.

_____

_____

_____

_____

_____

_____

_____

_____

_____

_____

How has the Lord shown you His extravagant love and how has He kissed you today?

_____

_____

_____

_____

_____

_____

_____

_____

Worship and thank Him for Who He is!

_____

_____

_____

_____

_____

_____

_____

_____

_____

Arise, My Bride, to a beautiful new day and a fresh start in Me!

Day 23

"How delightful is your love, my sister, my bride! How much more pleasing is your love than wine, and the fragrance of your perfume than any spice!" SS 4:10 (NIV)

Bridegroom: My Beauty, you told Me that My love was more delightful to you than wine. You said that My love was more delightful to you than anything this world has to offer. But I say to you that your love is more delightful to Me than wine - than anything this world has to offer! Your love, My Bride, is far greater than, much more pleasing and delightful than, sweeter than, and far superior to anything! Your love is more beautiful to Me than everything that My hands have created! My heart beats for you with passionate holy love! You say that in My presence is your fullness of joy! But I say to you that in your presence is My fullness of joy! Oh, the joy of being loved! I burn for you.

Bride: I look into Your eyes, my Beautiful King, and I see pure love! You love me! You want me! You even like me!!! The love I see in Your eyes melts my heart! You're happy about me! I see the twinkle in your eyes and it tells me that You are joyful about me and that I belong! You say that in my presence is fullness of joy! WOW! But I say that in Your presence, my King, is joy unspeakable and full of glory! I have never experienced ecstasy like this! My heart sings for joy at the thought of You! You want to be with me! This is too wonderful! This is too good to be true! You say my small weak love is more delightful and pleasing to you than anything this world has to offer! Wow! You really love the way I love You! You really love the way I love You in my own weak way. Oh, I can't help but fall all over again in love with You! Thank you for Your deep love! Thank you that it's true love! Thank You for this revelation! You do love me this way! I do bring joy to Your heart! I am wanted! I am loved! And I belong! Oh, what joy fills my heart in knowing I'm loved by You, My Beautiful King!

Scripture Reading: SS 4:10-11; SS 1:3; Ps. 16:11; I Peter 1:8

Encounter the Bridegroom God

Encounter the Bridegroom King as you read today's devotion (see Simple Steps to Encountering God and Sample Outline in Introduction). Continue your encounter with the Lord in your safe place. Journal as you share your hearts with one another.

Safe Place (describe)

_____
_____
_____

How can You, Papa, the Creator of the Universe, be happy about me? What about me makes You happy?

_____
_____
_____

Father, would You show me the twinkle in Your eyes when You think about me?

_____
_____
_____
_____

Bridegroom King, how much do You want me?

_____
_____
_____

I say that in Your presence is fullness of joy, Jesus (Ps. 16:11). How does my presence bring fullness of joy to Your heart?

_____
_____
_____
_____

Thank You God for Your amazing love! Thank You God for the delight and joy of being loved. Thank You for...

_____
_____

What truths are the Bridegroom/Papa/Holy Spirit speaking over you today? Write down these truths and speak them out loud as you see these truths in your imagination (i.e. He calls you beautiful, so see yourself as beautiful as you say out loud, "I'm beautiful!").

_____
_____
_____
_____
_____
_____
_____

What lies have you been believing? Ask the Lord to set you free from any deception and then focus on the Lord and His truth. Agree with God, and declare His life over you, as you speak/sing His truth.

_____
_____
_____
_____
_____
_____
_____

How does the Bridegroom God feel about you? See you?

_____
_____
_____
_____
_____
_____
_____

Who do you say the Lord is? (Matt. 16:13) Who you believe God to be will affect every area of your walk with Him. Speak the truth and see it!

_____
_____
_____
_____
_____
_____
_____

Who does the Lord say you are? What's the truth about your identity and your destiny? What you believe about yourself will affect every area of your walk with Him. Speak the truth out loud and see it.

_____
_____
_____
_____
_____
_____
_____
_____
_____
_____

How has the Lord shown you His extravagant love and how has He kissed you today?

_____
_____
_____
_____
_____
_____
_____
_____

Worship and thank Him for Who He is!

_____
_____
_____
_____
_____
_____
_____
_____
_____
_____

Arise, My Bride, and walk in your destiny! It's a new season!!

Day 24

"A garden enclosed is My sister, My spouse, a spring sealed up, a fountain sealed " SS 4:12 (NKJV) You are a garden locked up, my sister, my bride; you are a spring enclosed, a sealed fountain."
SS 4:12 (NIV)

Bridegroom: You are My private paradise! You are My oasis, My place of refreshment, joy, and delight! Within you, My waters of life spring up and satisfy Me. You are a locked garden for My pleasure alone and kept just for Me. The garden of your heart is a private place of rest and refreshment where I can come with delight as you minister to Me with your love, praise and worship. Your fragrance is intoxicating. My Bride, you are so beautiful, kind, gracious and generous. My heart beats with excitement when I think of your locked garden prepared for Me only. Thank you for My very own private paradise where I can rest in your love and share the secrets of My heart with you. Thank you that you care what I'm feeling and thinking. Thank you that you've prepared a place of beauty where I can rest. You are My beautiful, fragrant and colorful garden of love and joy!

Bride: Yes, I have prepared my heart for You! This locked garden paradise is for You and You only! Come and eat of the fruit of my life, my Bridegroom King. Come and rest and be refreshed in the garden of my heart! It's now Your garden for Your pleasure. Come into Your garden and share what's on Your heart. I desire only one thing and that's intimacy with You! My joy and longing is to sit at your feet and worship You, listening to every life-giving word of revelation and redemption that you speak! You are the most excellent One, the King of all Kings, and your lips have been anointed with grace! I love You, my Bridegroom King, Yeshua, and I always will!

Scripture Reading: SS 4:12-18; John 12:1-3; Luke 10:38-42; Ps. 45:2

Encounter the Bridegroom God

Encounter the Bridegroom King as you read today's devotion (see Simple Steps to Encountering God and Sample Outline in Introduction). Continue your encounter with the Lord in your safe place. Journal as you share your hearts with one another.

Safe Place (describe)

_____

_____

_____

Would You come into the garden of my heart, my Bridegroom King? Would You come into my locked garden that is prepared just for Your pleasure so that we can share our hearts with one another?

_____

_____

_____

_____

Jesus, come be refreshed and renewed in my garden of love for You. What's on Your heart, my King? What are You thinking and feeling?

_____

_____

_____

_____

Come and eat of the fruit of my life. It's all because of You, Jesus! It's all for You, Jesus!

_____

_____

_____

_____

Thank You, Yeshua, for Your life, light and love. Thank You that You invite me to sit at Your feet and receive from Your heart as I worship You. Thank You for...

_____

_____

_____

_____

What truths are the Bridegroom/Papa/Holy Spirit speaking over you today? Write down these truths and speak them out loud as you see these truths in your imagination (i.e. He calls you beautiful, so see yourself as beautiful as you say out loud, "I'm beautiful!").

_____

_____

_____

_____

_____

_____

_____

What lies have you been believing? Ask the Lord to set you free from any deception and then focus on the Lord and His truth. Agree with God, and declare His life over you, as you speak/sing His truth.

_____

_____

_____

_____

_____

_____

_____

How does the Bridegroom God feel about you? See you?

_____

_____

_____

_____

_____

_____

_____

Who do you say the Lord is? (Matt. 16:13) Who you believe God to be will affect every area of your walk with Him. Speak the truth and see it!

_____

_____

_____

_____

_____

_____

_____

Who does the Lord say you are? What's the truth about your identity and your destiny? What you believe about yourself will affect every area of your walk with Him. Speak the truth out loud and see it.

_____

_____

_____

_____

_____

_____

_____

_____

_____

_____

_____

How has the Lord shown you His extravagant love and how has He kissed you today?

_____

_____

_____

_____

_____

_____

_____

_____

Worship Him and thank Him for Who He is!

_____

_____

_____

_____

_____

_____

_____

_____

Arise, My Bride, and walk in your destiny! It's a new day!

Day 25

"He alone is my beloved. He shines in dazzling splendor yet is still so approachable - without equal as he stands above all others, outstanding among ten thousand!" SS 5:10 (tPt)

(Please read this whole passage of beautiful worship - SS 5:10-16.)

Bride: You, my Bridegroom King, are radiant and full of splendor, majesty and glory. I love You! You alone are my Lover! You are outstanding among the thousands. There is none like You. You are my First Love! You are perfect in all of Your ways, and Your leadership is flawless! You are pure gold! You see with perfect vision and perfect love! Your emotions are so fragrant and life-giving! Your lips are anointed with grace, and every word You speak brings life and redemption! You are powerful! Your works are supernatural and miraculous! You flow in healing, deliverance, freedom, love and so much more. You forgive all my sins and heal all my diseases! Your walk is solid, pure and perfect. Your appearance is beautiful and majestic, and Your fragrance is so delightful and life-giving. Your Word and Your love are sweetness itself! Intimacy with You is glorious! You are altogether lovely! There is none like You who gives all! I can't stop thinking about Your suffering love and sacrifice for me - the innocent for the guilty. I will forever say thank You! You are my Beloved and my closest Friend. Forever, I will remember Your love!

Bridegroom: Do you know the way you move Me? Your eyes of adoration and your voice in beautiful worship stun Me! You move My heart to ignite in burning flames of passionate fiery love as you worship Me in the midst of pain and persecution. My heart is touched as I see your desire to know Me and to know the fellowship of sharing in My sufferings. What love is this? I'm lovesick for you, My Bride!

Scripture Reading: SS 5:10-16; Ps. 45:2, 86:8, 103:3; Is. 53:5; Matt. 4:23

Encounter the Bridegroom God

Encounter the Bridegroom King as you read today's devotion (see Simple Steps to Encountering God and Sample Outline in Introduction). Continue your encounter with the Lord in your safe place. Journal as you share your hearts with one another.

Safe Place (describe)

_____
_____
_____

How does my worship move Your heart, Bridegroom King?

_____
_____
_____
_____
_____

What kind of love is this, that Your heart would ignite in burning flames of love when I worship You?

_____
_____
_____
_____
_____
_____
_____
_____
_____
_____

Thank You for Your suffering love and sacrifice for me - the innocent for the guilty. I will forever say thank You! Thank You for...

_____
_____
_____
_____
_____

What truths are the Bridegroom/Papa/Holy Spirit speaking over you today? Write down these truths and speak them out loud as you see these truths in your imagination (i.e. He calls you beautiful, so see yourself as beautiful as you say out loud, "I'm beautiful!").

_____
_____
_____
_____
_____
_____
_____

What lies have you been believing? Ask the Lord to set you free from any deception and then focus on the Lord and His truth. Agree with God, and declare His life over you, as you speak/sing His truth.

_____
_____
_____
_____
_____
_____

How does the Bridegroom God feel about you? See you?

_____
_____
_____
_____
_____
_____

Who do you say the Lord is? (Matt. 16:13) Who you believe God to be will affect every area of your walk with Him. Speak the truth and see it!

_____
_____
_____
_____
_____
_____
_____

Who does the Lord say you are? What's the truth about your identity and your destiny? What you believe about yourself will affect every area of your walk with Him. Speak the truth out loud and see it.

_____
_____
_____
_____
_____
_____
_____
_____
_____
_____
_____

How has the Lord shown you His extravagant love and how has He kissed you today?

_____
_____
_____
_____
_____
_____
_____
_____
_____

Worship and thank Him for Who He is!

_____
_____
_____
_____
_____
_____
_____
_____
_____
_____

Arise, My Bride, and walk in My love! It's a new day!

Day 26

*"I am my lover's and my lover is mine."
SS 6:3 (NIV) "I am my beloved's, And my
beloved is mine." SS 6:3 (NKJ) "He is
within me - I am his garden of delight. I
have him fully and now he fully has me!"
SS 6:3 (tPt)*

Bride: Yes, You live within me! You feast from my garden of delights! You have given Yourself to me fully and held nothing back. I give myself to You fully as well. I keep nothing hidden from You, my Love. I love You, My King, wider, longer, higher and deeper than I can comprehend, for You are within me and it's Your love flowing between us! It takes God to love God! We are one, with no veil between us! I am Yours, and You are mine! Oh, the ecstasy that floods my heart as I see the delight in Your eyes when You gaze at me and hear the joy in Your voice as You sing over me. I belong to You, and You belong to me. Forever we will be one!

Bridegroom: You are a rare beauty! Your love melts and moves My heart in ways you will never know! My heart pounds with love for you. The river of love that flows from My heart to yours is wider, longer, higher and deeper than you could ever imagine! Forever we are one, never alone or lonely, Me in you and you in Me! Together forever! We delight ourselves in one another and bubble over with joy unspeakable and full of glory as we partner together in perfect love! No eye has seen, no ear has heard, no mind has conceived what I have prepared for those who love Me, even now in this life.

Scripture Reading: SS 6:3; I Peter 1:8; I Cor. 2:9; Eph. 3:17-18

Encounter the Bridegroom God

Encounter the Bridegroom King as you read today's devotion (see Simple Steps to Encountering God and Sample Outline in Introduction). Continue your encounter with the Lord in your safe place. Journal as you share your hearts with one another.

Safe Place (describe)

_____

_____

_____

Bridegroom King, would You reveal to me the delight in Your eyes as You gaze at me? Would you let me hear the joy in Your voice as You sing over me?

_____

_____

_____

_____

_____

_____

_____

_____

_____

What kinds of unseen, unheard of and undiscovered things have You prepared, Bridegroom King, for those who love You?

_____

_____

_____

_____

_____

_____

Thank You for the river of love flowing from within Your heart! Thank You that I belong to You! Thank You for...

_____

_____

_____

_____

What truths are the Bridegroom/Papa/Holy Spirit speaking over you today? Write down these truths and speak them out loud as you see these truths in your imagination (i.e. He calls you beautiful, so see yourself as beautiful as you say out loud, "I'm beautiful!").

_____
_____
_____
_____
_____
_____
_____

What lies have you been believing? Ask the Lord to set you free from any deception and then focus on the Lord and His truth. Agree with God, and declare His life over you, as you speak/sing His truth.

_____
_____
_____
_____
_____
_____

How does the Bridegroom God feel about you? See you?

_____
_____
_____
_____
_____
_____
_____

Who do you say the Lord is? (Matt. 16:13) Who you believe God to be will affect every area of your walk with Him. Speak the truth and see it!

_____
_____
_____
_____
_____
_____
_____

Who does the Lord say you are? What's the truth about your identity and your destiny? What you believe about yourself will affect every area of your walk with Him. Speak the truth out loud and see it.

_____
_____
_____
_____
_____
_____
_____
_____
_____
_____

How has the Lord shown you His extravagant love and how has He kissed you today?

_____
_____
_____
_____
_____
_____
_____
_____

Worship and thank Him for Who He is!

_____
_____
_____
_____
_____
_____
_____
_____
_____

Arise, My Bride, and walk in your destiny! It's a new day!

Day 27

"O my beloved, you are lovely...More pleasing than any pleasure, more delightful than any delight, you have ravished my heart...Turn your eyes from me; I can't take it anymore! I can't resist the passion of those eyes that I adore."
SS 6:4-5 (tPt)

Bridegroom: My Beloved, you have undone My heart! You are beautiful, lovely, and majestic, My Love! There is none like you. Not one! You love Me even though I lifted My manifest presence from you (but of course have never left you), and you love Me even though you have experienced persecution from your brothers in the church! How beautiful! You are still in love with Me in spite of your ministry being taken from you. I'm undone! Look away from Me! Your eyes, they overwhelm Me! I am captured by your extravagant love! You, My Dove, have conquered My heart! No one can conquer Me, but you have! I'm overcome by your love, and I'm overcome with love for you!

Bride: You, my Dearest Darling, have undone my heart! It's only because Your great love has conquered me that I could walk as an overcomer through the hurt and pain of this life. Where else could I go? You are the life-giving King of LOVE! You have the words of eternal life! You are my very great reward. You have won my heart! One thing I ask, this is what I seek, that I may dwell in Your house all the days of my life to gaze upon Your beauty and to seek You in Your temple, my Bridegroom King. You are my one thing! You are my one desire! I choose You, Yeshua, forever! There is no end to the depth of Your beauty, majesty, glory and splendor! You are not a boring God! I live fascinated in You, my Bridegroom King, now and for all eternity! I choose You! I love You, now and always!

Scripture Reading: SS 6:4-5; Gen. 15:1; John 6:68; Ps. 27:4

Encounter the Bridegroom God

Encounter the Bridegroom King as you read today's devotion (see Simple Steps to Encountering God and Sample Outline in Introduction). Continue your encounter with the Lord in your safe place. Journal as you share your hearts with one another.

Safe Place (describe)

_____

_____

_____

How could You be overcome with my love?

_____

_____

_____

_____

_____

_____

Would you heal the pain in my heart?

_____

_____

_____

Who can conquer Your heart, my Bridegroom King?

_____

_____

_____

_____

_____

_____

Thank You, God, that You are overwhelmed by my gaze of love upon You. Thank You that You love me totally and completely! Thank You for...

_____

_____

_____

What truths are the Bridegroom/Papa/Holy Spirit speaking over you today? Write down these truths and speak them out loud as you see these truths in your imagination (i.e. He calls you beautiful, so see yourself as beautiful as you say out loud, "I'm beautiful!").

_____

_____

_____

_____

_____

_____

_____

What lies have you been believing? Ask the Lord to set you free from any deception and then focus on the Lord and His truth. Agree with God, and declare His life over you, as you speak/sing His truth.

_____

_____

_____

_____

_____

_____

How does the Bridegroom God feel about you? See you?

_____

_____

_____

_____

_____

_____

Who do you say the Lord is? (Matt. 16:13) Who you believe God to be will affect every area of your walk with Him. Speak the truth and see it!

_____

_____

_____

_____

_____

_____

Who does the Lord say you are? What's the truth about your identity and your destiny? What you believe about yourself will affect every area of your walk with Him. Speak the truth out loud and see it.

_____
_____
_____
_____
_____
_____
_____
_____
_____
_____
_____
_____

How has the Lord shown you His extravagant love and how has He kissed you today?

_____
_____
_____
_____
_____
_____
_____
_____

Worship and thank Him for Who He is!

_____
_____
_____
_____
_____
_____
_____
_____

Arise, My Bride, and walk in your destiny! It's a new day!

Day 28

"Who is this woman? She is like the sunrise in all of its glory. She is as beautiful as the moon. She is as bright as the sun..." SS 6:10 (NIRV)

Bridegroom: Who are you? Look at you! You are absolutely stunning! Your beauty takes My breath away! You shine like the sun in all its dazzling brilliance! Your head and hair emit pure bright light! Your eyes are full of blazing fire! Your voice sounds like mighty rushing waters! You look and sound like Me! You are as beautiful and as bright as the moon, shining in the darkness of this fallen world to bring in the harvest! You are wise and shine like the brightness of the heavens, leading many to righteousness. You are as majestic as the stars shining in all their glory, a guiding light to the hurting and lost. You are terrifying to the enemy as you overcome him by the blood of the Lamb, My blood, and the word of your testimony. And you, My Bride, are fearless in the face of death. You are astonishing! I'm hopelessly in love with you! You are unrivaled in beauty and strength. You are beyond compare and without equal. You are My favorite one, My Dove! I'm in love with you!

Bride: It's only because of You! Your extravagant love has overcome the fear in my life! You are the One who has done this! I'm beautiful only because of You and what You did for me at the cross! Thank You for Your blood! Thank You for setting me free from fear by loving me with Your amazing love. Thank You that Your love has conquered fear and driven it out so that I can partner with You to bring Your life, light and love to this struggling world! Thank You that You have opened my eyes and given me vision to see the joy of what's ahead as we run together. I am FREE! Your love has set me FREE TO BE ME and to walk in the hope of Your calling, Your destiny for my life! Thank You! Thank You! Thank You!

Scripture Reading: SS 6:10-13; Rev. 1:14-15; Dan. 12:3; Rev. 12:11; Eph. 1:18

Encounter the Bridegroom God

Encounter the Bridegroom King as you read today's devotion (see Simple Steps to Encountering God and Sample Outline in Introduction). Continue your encounter with the Lord in your safe place. Journal as you share your hearts with one another.

Safe Place (describe)

_____

_____

_____

Who are You, my beautiful God, Who extravagantly loves me beyond my wildest imagination?

_____

_____

_____

_____

_____

Oh, Jesus, how am I being transformed from glory to glory into Your image? How am I maturing in my walk with You?

_____

_____

_____

_____

_____

_____

_____

_____

Thank You, Lord, for Your extravagant love that has overcome the fear in my life! Thank You for setting me free from fear through Your amazing love. Thank You for...

_____

_____

_____

_____

What truths are the Bridegroom/Papa/Holy Spirit speaking over you today? Write down these truths and speak them out loud as you see these truths in your imagination (i.e. He calls you beautiful, so see yourself as beautiful as you say out loud, "I'm beautiful!").

_____

_____

_____

_____

_____

_____

_____

What lies have you been believing? Ask the Lord to set you free from any deception and then focus on the Lord and His truth. Agree with God, and declare His life over you, as you speak/sing His truth.

_____

_____

_____

_____

_____

_____

_____

How does the Bridegroom God feel about you? See you?

_____

_____

_____

_____

_____

_____

_____

Who do you say the Lord is? (Matt. 16:13) Who you believe God to be will affect every area of your walk with Him. Speak the truth and see it!

_____

_____

_____

_____

_____

_____

_____

Who does the Lord say you are? What's the truth about your identity and your destiny? What you believe about yourself will affect every area of your walk with Him. Speak the truth out loud and see it.

_____
_____
_____
_____
_____
_____
_____
_____
_____
_____
_____

How has the Lord shown you His extravagant love and how has He kissed you today?

_____
_____
_____
_____
_____
_____
_____
_____
_____
_____
_____

Worship Him and thank Him! for Who He is!

_____
_____
_____
_____
_____
_____
_____
_____

Arise, My Bride, and walk in your destiny! It's a new beginning!

Day 29

"I belong to my lover, and His desire is for me." SS 7:10 (NIV) "Now I know that I am filled with my beloved and all his desires are fulfilled in me." SS 7:10 (tPt)

Bride: I belong to You! I'm Yours! I belong with You, by Your side! What joy! I belong to You, my Beloved, and You belong to me forever. I abandon myself to You because I know that everything You choose for my life is for my good! You are a safe Savior Who only wants what's best for me! I trust You and surrender my life to You, My Beloved. I know that Your desire is for me! Pleasing You, Jesus, is my greatest pleasure! I know who I am! I am the one that fulfills all Your desires! I'm the one You long for! You want me! I am Your gorgeous rose, Your glorious inheritance. I'm Your beauty! You see me maturing and beginning to look more like You as I am transformed into Your image. You chose me! Yes! You chose me! And I choose You! I'm letting go of my past and laying everything down for the priceless privilege and surpassing greatness of knowing You, Yeshua, and becoming more intimately acquainted with You. I'm in You, and You're in me. The joy that we share together as Bride and Groom will forever burst forth in fountains of flaming love. You are everything I've ever wanted, everything I've ever longed for, and everything I've ever desired! It's all found in You, my King! All my longings and desires are fulfilled in YOU! Oh, the joy of being loved! You have swept me off my feet!

Bridegroom: You are a stunning Beauty without rival! Your intoxicating fragrance floods me inside and out, and the love song you are singing washes over Me wave upon wave. I'm resting and receiving in your garden of joy! Your beauty is unequaled! You belong to Me, and I belong to you, and My heart is yours! All My longings and desires are fulfilled in you! You are everything I've ever wanted, everything I've ever longed for and everything I've ever desired. It's all found in you, My Sweetheart! Oh, the joy of being loved! I'm "in love" with you!

Scripture Reading: SS 7:1-13; Rom. 8:29; Eph. 1:4; Phil. 3:8

Encounter the Bridegroom God

Encounter the Bridegroom King as you read today's devotion (see Simple Steps to Encountering God and Sample Outline in Introduction). Continue your encounter with the Lord in your safe place. Journal as you share your hearts with one another.

Safe Place (describe)

_____
_____
_____

If I abandon everything to You, Jesus, will You choose what's best for my life? What do you want me to surrender to You today, Jesus?

_____
_____
_____
_____
_____
_____
_____

How safe are You, Jesus? Can I trust You completely?

_____
_____
_____
_____
_____
_____
_____
_____
_____

Thank You, Bridegroom King, that You are everything I've ever wanted, everything I've ever longed for and everything I've ever needed. Thank You for...

_____
_____
_____

What truths are the Bridegroom/Papa/Holy Spirit speaking over you today? Write down these truths and speak them out loud as you see these truths in your imagination (i.e. He calls you beautiful, so see yourself as beautiful as you say out loud, "I'm beautiful!").

_____
_____
_____
_____
_____
_____
_____

What lies have you been believing? Ask the Lord to set you free from any deception and then focus on the Lord and His truth. Agree with God, and declare His life over you, as you speak/sing His truth.

_____
_____
_____
_____
_____
_____
_____

How does the Bridegroom God feel about you? See you?

_____
_____
_____
_____
_____
_____
_____

Who do you say the Lord is? (Matt. 16:13) Who you believe God to be will affect every area of your walk with Him. Speak the truth and see it!

_____
_____
_____
_____
_____
_____
_____

Who does the Lord say you are? What's the truth about your identity and your destiny? What you believe about yourself will affect every area of your walk with Him. Speak the truth out loud and see it.

_____
_____
_____
_____
_____
_____
_____
_____

How has the Lord shown you His extravagant love and how has He kissed you today?

_____
_____
_____
_____
_____
_____
_____
_____

Worship Him and thank Him for Who He is!

_____
_____
_____
_____
_____
_____
_____
_____
_____
_____
_____
_____
_____

Arise, My Bride, and experience My joy and delight over you!

Day 30

"Who is this coming up from the wilderness, leaning on her beloved?" SS 8:5 (NKJV)

Bridegroom: Oh, wow! Who is this beauty coming up from the desert leaning? Look at her! She's a leaning lover! You're absolutely stunning! You're all glorious! You've learned to lean on Me! You've learned to receive courage, strength, life, love and everything from Me, and to walk out your destiny with authority from that place of intimacy. You're no longer going at it on your own, but you're leaning on Me! I'm so proud of you! You didn't quit! You never gave up! You won! Love won! What a lover! We are one! We won! I will never leave you or forsake you. I am always here for you. I will never reject or abandon you! Lean not on your own understanding but lean on Me always and forever, for when you are weak, then I am strong! My grace is sufficient for you, for my strength is made perfect in weakness. I am in love with you, even in your weakness, and I'm pouring out my grace upon you. My power is made perfect in weakness! In everything give Me thanks. For I take the foolish things of this world to confound the wise. I choose the insignificant and the nobodies of this world to bring glory and honor to My name! No longer will they call you Rejected or Forsaken, but you shall be called My Delight! I love you, and I choose you!

Bride: Oh, how I love You! You have captured my heart! Thank You for bringing me through this difficult wilderness! I will forever praise and adore You. I worship You and will sing of Your love forever! When I am weak, my Bridegroom King, then You are strong! Your grace is sufficient for me. You were there with me in it all. You never left my side! You never rejected or abandoned me. Thank You! As I walked and limped in humility by Your side, Your grace came flooding in to empower me to fulfill all that You've called me to! Thank You for Your love and grace! Thank You for Your vision and destiny for me. Thank You for choosing me! I will always remember Your faithful love!

Scripture Reading: SS 8:1-5; Prov. 3:5; 2Cor.12:9; I Cor.1:27; Is. 62:4

Encounter the Bridegroom God

Encounter the Bridegroom King as you read today's devotion (see Simple Steps to Encountering God and Sample Outline in Introduction). Continue your encounter with the Lord in your safe place. Journal as you share your hearts with one another.

Safe Place (describe)

_____
_____
_____

How do you want me to lean on You, Lord? Is Your grace truly sufficient for me in all situations?

_____
_____
_____
_____
_____

How does thanking You in all circumstances help me?

_____
_____
_____
_____

My Beautiful Bridegroom God, are You really proud of me? Can You show me?

_____
_____
_____
_____
_____

ThanK You, Bridegroom King, that I am not rejected but I'm accepted by You! Thank you for...

_____
_____
_____
_____

What truths are the Bridegroom/Papa/Holy Spirit speaking over you today? Write down these truths and speak them out loud as you see these truths in your imagination (i.e. He calls you beautiful, so see yourself as beautiful as you say out loud, "I'm beautiful!").

_____

_____

_____

_____

_____

_____

_____

What lies have you been believing? Ask the Lord to set you free from any deception and then focus on the Lord and His truth. Agree with God, and declare His life over you, as you speak/sing His truth.

_____

_____

_____

_____

_____

_____

How does the Bridegroom God feel about you? See you?

_____

_____

_____

_____

_____

_____

Who do you say the Lord is? (Matt. 16:13) Who you believe God to be will affect every area of your walk with Him. Speak the truth and see it!

_____

_____

_____

_____

_____

_____

Who does the Lord say you are? What's the truth about your identity and your destiny? What you believe about yourself will affect every area of your walk with Him. Speak the truth out loud and see it.

_____
_____
_____
_____
_____
_____
_____
_____

How has the Lord shown you His extravagant love and how has He kissed you today?

_____
_____
_____
_____
_____
_____
_____
_____

Worship Him and thank Him for Who He is!

_____
_____
_____
_____
_____
_____
_____
_____
_____
_____
_____
_____

Arise, My Bride, and walk in your destiny! It's a new day!

Day 31

"Place me like a seal over your heart, like a seal on your arm; for love...burns like blazing fire, like a mighty flame."
SS 8:6 (NIV)

Bridegroom: My Bride, I invite you to place My fiery burning love over your heart, and seal your heart forever in My glorious passion. Set Me over your entire being, including your ministry, and receive My seal over every area of your life that you might burn with My fiery passionate love inside and out. Let Me seal you and your destiny forever! Let us freely dance with joy in My seal of blazing love! I give you all My heart, all that I am and all that I have! This is My invitation of love to you! You are chosen! Will you choose Me? Will you have all of Me? Will you love and cherish Me forever? Will you marry Me?

Bride: Yes, I will marry You, my Beautiful King! I invite You to come and seal my heart in Your fiery passionate love that I would burn forever with holy desire for You. Come and seal my entire being, spirit, soul and body, in Your passion, that I would be ablaze with love for You, even when ministry or life gets hard. Seal me in Your fire so that many waters of pain, rejection, persecution, sin, and selfishness would never wash away Your love in my heart. Your love means more to me than life itself! Oh, the joy of being loved by You, the Creator of the universe, and the greatest Lover of all time! I'm Yours, and I surrender all! I receive Your gift of life and love! I receive all that You are and all that You have, and, in return, I give You my gift of love and all that I am and all that I have! You are everything I've ever wanted, everything I've ever needed, everything I've ever longed for! I love You, and I trust You. I say, "Yes," I will dance joyfully with You through life! I will go where You go. I will obey your lead. I will dance with You on the mountaintops, and I will dance with You in the valleys below. I say, "Yes," I will marry You! "Yes," I will ascend the mountain of intimacy with You! I love and cherish You, and I'm Yours forever!

Scripture Reading: SS 8:6-14; Ps. 63:3; Ruth 1:16

Encounter the Bridegroom God

Encounter the Bridegroom King as you read today's devotion (see Simple Steps to Encountering God and Sample Outline in Introduction). Continue your encounter with the Lord in your safe place. Journal as you share your hearts with one another.

Safe Place (describe)

_____
_____
_____

Would You come and place Your fiery burning seal of love over my heart, my Bridegroom King? Would you let me feel Your love for me?

_____
_____
_____
_____
_____
_____

Would You come and place Your passionate burning seal of love over my entire being and my destiny?

_____
_____
_____
_____
_____
_____
_____
_____

Thank You for loving me, Yeshua! Thank You for sealing me in Your love. I will burn with love for You forever and ever! Thank You for...

_____
_____
_____
_____
_____
_____
_____

What truths are the Bridegroom/Papa/Holy Spirit speaking over you today? Write down these truths and speak them out loud as you see these truths in your imagination (i.e. He calls you beautiful, so see yourself as beautiful as you say out loud, "I'm beautiful!").

_____
_____
_____
_____
_____
_____
_____

What lies have you been believing? Ask the Lord to set you free from any deception and then focus on the Lord and His truth. Agree with God, and declare His life over you, as you speak/sing His truth.

_____
_____
_____
_____
_____
_____

How does the Bridegroom God feel about you? See you?

_____
_____
_____
_____
_____
_____

Who do you say the Lord is? (Matt. 16:13) Who you believe God to be will affect every area of your walk with Him. Speak the truth and see it!

_____
_____
_____
_____
_____
_____

Who does the Lord say you are? What's the truth about your identity and your destiny? What you believe about yourself will affect every area of your walk with Him. Speak the truth out loud and see it.

_____
_____
_____
_____
_____
_____
_____
_____
_____
_____
_____

How has the Lord shown you His extravagant love and how has He kissed you today?

_____
_____
_____
_____
_____
_____
_____
_____
_____

Worship Him and thank Him for Who He is!

_____
_____
_____
_____
_____
_____
_____
_____
_____

Arise, My Bride, in the joy of being loved and fulfill your destiny!

An Invitation from the Bridegroom

Come and dance with Me to the Song of all Songs. Come and join the dance of the Trinity - the Father, the Son and Holy Spirit. I invite you to join Us in the divine dance that My Father, Holy Spirit and I are dancing in. Come and center your life in ME. Come and receive Our perfect love in the divine dance. Our hearts long to give to you, to pour Our love into your heart, and to honor you as We (Trinity) love and honor each other perfectly! Come, and let go of self, earthly things, worries, and cares and dance with Us in the divine romance. Don't dance the dance of the enemy or the dance of self! Focus your heart on Me and the things of earth will grow strangely dim. Get lost in Our love and joy over you and repent and die to self! I created you to give you My endless love. You were created for love! Come and be ONE with Us! Come and be ONE with Me! Let Me give to you My life, light and love. Encounter Me. Experience Me. Focus on Me! Hear Me singing the greatest love song of all over you. Dance with Me to the most beautiful love song ever written! Let Me hold you close in the divine dance. You are welcomed! You are invited! You are wanted, cherished and loved. There is nothing like the joy of knowing you are loved! You are Mine, and I am yours. Forever we will be united as one in love! Come join the eternal romance of all the ages. Come, join the divine dance and experience *The Joy of Being Loved!*

I Am in Love with You

(Song from the Lord 8/23/18)
Denise Siemens

Bride:

I am in love with You
You are my everything
You are my LOVE
You are my JOY
You are my Bridegroom King.

Yes, I will dance with You
Throughout all of life.
I am Your LOVE
I am Your JOY
I am Your Fearless Bride

So let us run on the mountains
Roar in the heavens
And sing over nations of Your healing LOVE

I am Yours and Your desire is for me
We're one in Your Chuppah cloud of glory.

Bridegroom King:

I am in love with you.
You are My treasured prize
You are My LOVE
You are My JOY
You're My delightful Bride.

We share an intimacy
Which gives authority
My heart's your home
Your heart's My own
Walk in your destiny.

So let us run on the mountains
Roar in the heavens
And sing over nations of My healing LOVE

I am yours and your desire is for ME
Together we will bring My Kingdom's glory!

Made in the USA
Columbia, SC
26 May 2019